perfect
baking

Bath · New York · Singapore · Hong Kong · Cologne · Delhi · Melbourne

This edition published by Parragon in 2008

Parragon Publishing
Queen Street House
4 Queen Street
Bath BA1 1HE, UK

Copyright © Parragon Books Ltd 2007
Designed by Terry Jeavons & Company

ISBN 978-1-4075-2621-8

Printed in Indonesia

This book uses imperial, metric, and US cup measurements. Follow the same units of measurement throughout; do not mix imperial and metric. All spoon measurements are level, unless otherwise stated: teaspoons are assumed to be 5ml, and tablespoons are assumed to be 15ml. Unless otherwise stated, milk is assumed to be whole, eggs and individual fruits such as bananas are medium, and pepper is freshly ground black pepper.

Recipes using raw or very lightly cooked eggs should be avoided by infants, the elderly, pregnant women, convalescents, and anyone suffering from an illness. Pregnant and breast-feeding women are advised to avoid eating peanuts and peanut products.

Assortment of Baked Goods © James Porter/Brand X/Corbis

perfect baking

introduction

Baking is without any doubt the most rewarding of culinary experiences. To mix together the most unpromising-looking collection of ingredients, put them in an oven, and have them emerge as a truly delicious creation is nothing short of a miracle!

No wonder, then, that there is something of a mystery to the whole process that is often daunting to an inexperienced cook. In reality, however, it's nowhere near as difficult as it might appear to bake a sumptuous large cake, a melt-in-the-mouth muffin, your favorite pie, a loaf of bread to serve fresh from the oven, or an elegant savory tart—and these are just a few examples of the

wonderful baking recipes you will find in this book!

There are several items of kitchen equipment that are worth investing in if you are planning to make baking a regular event. A selection of baking pans is a must—cookie sheets and tart pans, as well as round and square cake pans of various sizes, including one or two of the "springform" type to facilitate the removal of large cakes, tortes, and cheesecakes.

Apart from this, a couple of generously sized mixing bowls, some wooden spoons, and perhaps a hand-held electric mixer will be enough to get you started. A more expensive item of equipment that will pay for itself in no time is a multipurpose food mixer. The different attachments will enable you to mix cake batters and pie doughs, whisk egg whites, whip cream, and knead bread dough with speed and efficiency. In the past, of course, cooks had no such gadgets to help them out, and there is a certain satisfaction in

doing all of the above tasks by hand—kneading bread dough for ten minutes is guaranteed to relieve tension as well as produce a fabulous result!

Choose your favorite recipe, mix it with confidence—and wait for the golden moment when you can bite into it!

cakes & gateaux

Although a store-bought cake is convenient and usually very good, a home-baked cake is so much better, perhaps because a little bit of the soul of the cook goes into it along with the other ingredients! If it doesn't come out looking absolutely perfect, it really doesn't matter—this just adds to its charm.

Different cakes suit different occasions, and you'll find a good cross-section here. For serving with morning coffee, try Gingerbread, Sticky Ginger Marmalade Loaf, or Date & Walnut Loaf—these cakes improve with keeping, so can be wrapped in foil and stored in an airtight container for a few days. For an afternoon treat with tea, Sponge Cake, German Chocolate & Hazelnut Cake, Caribbean Coconut Cake, Honey Spiced Cake, Rich Fruit Cake, and Banana & Lime Cake are perfect.

Some cakes make fabulous late-evening desserts—try a melting Torta de Cielo, fragrant Moroccan Orange & Almond Cake, moist Apple Streusel Cake, or spicy Pear & Ginger Cake. Add a spoonful of whipped cream, ice cream, sour cream, or thick yogurt, if you like.

And for those really special occasions? Chocolate Fudge Cake, Mocha Layer Cake, Coffee Caramel Cake, Chocolate Truffle Torte, Chocolate Cherry Gateau—you'll want to try them all!

chocolate fudge cake

ingredients

SERVES 8

6 oz/175 g unsalted butter,
   softened, plus extra for
   greasing
6 oz/175 g/scant 1 cup golden
   superfine sugar
3 eggs, beaten
3 tbsp dark corn syrup
$1^{1}/_{2}$ oz/40 g/$^{1}/_{3}$ cup ground
   almonds
6 oz/175 g/$1^{1}/_{4}$ cups self-
   rising flour
pinch of salt
$1^{1}/_{2}$ oz/40 g/$^{1}/_{3}$ cup
   unsweetened cocoa

frosting

8 oz/225 g plain chocolate,
   broken into pieces
2 oz/55 g/$^{1}/_{3}$ cup dark
   muscovado sugar
8 oz/225 g unsalted butter,
   diced
5 tbsp evaporated milk
$^{1}/_{2}$ tsp vanilla extract

method

1 Grease and line the bottom of 2 x 8-inch/ 20-cm round cake pans. To make the frosting, place the chocolate, sugar, butter, evaporated milk, and vanilla extract in a heavy-bottom pan. Heat gently, stirring constantly, until melted. Pour into a bowl and let cool. Cover and let chill in the retrigerator for 1 hour, or until spreadable.

2 Place the butter and sugar in a bowl and beat together until light and fluffy. Gradually beat in the eggs. Stir in the syrup and ground almonds. Sift the flour, salt, and cocoa into a separate bowl, then fold into the mixture. Add a little water, if necessary, to make a dropping consistency. Spoon the mixture into the prepared pans and bake in a preheated oven, 350°F/180°C, for 30–35 minutes, or until springy to the touch and a skewer inserted in the center comes out clean.

3 Leave the cakes in the pans for 5 minutes, then turn out onto wire racks to cool completely. When the cakes are cold, sandwich them together with half the frosting. Spread the remaining frosting over the top and sides of the cake, swirling it to give a frosted appearance.

gingerbread

ingredients

MAKES 12–16 PIECES

1 lb/450 g/3^1/$_2$ cups
  all-purpose flour
3 tsp baking powder
1 tsp baking soda
3 tsp ground ginger
6 oz/175 g butter
6 oz/175 g/^{3}/$_4$ cup soft
  brown sugar
6 oz/175 g/^{1}/$_2$ cup black
  molasses
6 oz/175 g/^{1}/$_2$ cup dark
  corn syrup
1 egg, beaten
10 fl oz/300 ml/1^1/$_4$ cups milk

method

1 Line a 9-inch/23-cm square cake pan, 2 inches/5 cm deep, with parchment paper.

2 Sift the flour, baking powder, baking soda, and ginger into a large mixing bowl.

3 Place the butter, sugar, molasses, and syrup in a medium pan and heat over low heat until the butter has melted and the sugar dissolved. Let cool a little.

4 Mix the beaten egg with the milk and add to the cooled syrup mixture. Add the liquid ingredients to the flour mixture and beat well using a wooden spoon until the mixture is smooth and glossy.

5 Pour the mixture into the prepared pan and bake in the center of a preheated oven, 325°F/160°C, for 1^1/$_2$ hours until well risen and just firm to the touch.

6 Remove from the oven and let cool in the pan. When cool, remove the cake from the pan, with the lining paper. Overwrap with foil and place in an airtight container for up to 1 week to allow the flavors to mature. Cut into wedges to serve.

sticky ginger marmalade loaf

ingredients

SERVES 10

6 oz/175 g butter, softened,
   plus extra for greasing
4^1/$_2$ oz/125 g/^{1}/$_3$ cup ginger
   marmalade
6 oz/175 g/scant 1 cup
   brown sugar
3 eggs, beaten
8 oz/225 g/generous
   1^1/$_2$ cups self-rising flour
^{1}/$_2$ tsp baking powder
1 tsp ground ginger
3^1/$_2$ oz/100 g/^{2}/$_3$ cup coarsely
   chopped pecans

method

1 Grease and line the bottom and ends of a 2-lb/900-g loaf pan. Place 1 tablespoon of the ginger marmalade in a small pan and reserve. Place the remaining marmalade in a bowl with the butter, sugar, and eggs.

2 Sift in the flour, baking powder, and ground ginger and beat together until smooth. Stir in three-fourths of the nuts. Spoon the mixture into the prepared loaf pan and smooth the top. Sprinkle with the remaining nuts and bake in a preheated oven, 350°F/180°C, for 1 hour, or until well risen and a skewer inserted into the center comes out clean.

3 Let cool in the pan for 10 minutes, then turn out and peel off the lining paper. Transfer to a wire rack to cool until warm. Set the pan of reserved marmalade over low heat to warm, then brush over the loaf and serve in slices.

carrot cake

ingredients

MAKES 16 PIECES

2 eggs

6 oz/175 g/^{3}/$_4$ cup molasses
　　sugar

7 fl oz/200 ml/scant 1 cup
　　sunflower oil

7 oz/200 g/generous 1^1/$_3$ cups
　　coarsely grated carrots

8 oz/225 g/2 cups all-purpose
　　whole wheat flour

1 tsp baking soda

2 tsp ground cinnamon

whole nutmeg, grated
　　(about 1 tsp)

4 oz/115 g/1 cup roughly
　　chopped walnuts

topping

4 oz/115 g/^{1}/$_2$ cup half-fat
　　cream cheese

4 tbsp butter, softened

3 oz/85 g/^{3}/$_4$ cup
　　confectioners' sugar

1 tsp grated lemon rind

1 tsp grated orange rind

method

1 In a mixing bowl, beat the eggs until well blended and add the sugar and oil. Mix well. Add the grated carrot, sift in the flour, baking soda, and spices, then add the walnuts. Mix everything together until well incorporated.

2 Spread the mixture into the prepared cake pan and bake in the center of a preheated oven, 375°F/190°C, for 40–50 minutes until the cake is nicely risen, firm to the touch, and has begun to shrink away slightly from the edge of the pan. Remove from the oven and let cool in the pan until just warm, then turn out onto a cooling rack.

3 To make the topping, put all the ingredients into a mixing bowl and beat together for 2–3 minutes until really smooth.

4 When the cake is completely cold, spread with the topping, smooth over with a fork, and let firm up a little before cutting into 16 portions. Store in an airtight container in a cool place for up to 1 week.

banana & chocolate loaf

ingredients

SERVES 8

4 oz/115 g butter, softened,
   plus extra for greasing

2 ripe bananas

3 oz/85 g/scant $^1/_2$ cup golden
   superfine sugar

2 eggs

7 oz/220 g/scant $1^1/_2$ cups
   self-rising flour

1 oz/25 g/$^1/_4$ cup
   unsweetened cocoa

1 tsp baking powder

1–2 tbsp milk

$3^1/_2$ oz/100 g/generous $^1/_2$ cup
   semisweet chocolate chips

butter, to serve (optional)

method

1 Grease and line a 2-lb/900-g loaf pan. Peel the bananas and place in a large bowl. Mash with a fork.

2 Add the butter, sugar, and eggs, then sift the flour, unsweetened cocoa, and baking powder into the bowl. Beat vigorously until smooth, adding enough milk to give a reluctant dropping consistency. Stir in the chocolate chips.

3 Spoon the mixture into the prepared pan and bake in a preheated oven, 350°F/180°C, for 50–60 minutes, or until well risen and the tip of a knife inserted in the center comes out clean. Let stand in the pan for 5 minutes, then turn out onto a wire rack to cool completely. Serve sliced, with or without butter.

date & walnut loaf

ingredients

SERVES 10

6 oz/175 g butter, plus extra
for greasing

8 oz/225 g/scant 1^1/$_3$ cups
pitted dates, chopped into
small pieces

grated rind and juice
of 1 orange

2 fl oz/50 ml/scant ^{1}/$_4$ cup
water

6 oz/175g/scant 1 cup
brown sugar

3 eggs, beaten

3 oz/85 g/^{2}/$_3$ cup self-rising
whole wheat flour

3 oz/85 g/^{2}/$_3$ cup
self-rising flour

2 oz/55 g/^{1}/$_3$ cup chopped
walnuts

8 walnut halves

orange zest, to decorate

method

1 Grease and line the bottom and ends of a 2-lb/900-g loaf pan. Place the dates in a pan with the orange rind and juice and water and cook over medium heat for 5 minutes, stirring, or until a soft purée has formed.

2 Place the butter and sugar in a bowl and beat together until light and fluffy. Gradually beat in the eggs, then sift in the flours and fold in with the chopped walnuts. Spread one third of the mixture over the bottom of the prepared loaf pan and spread half the date purée over the top.

3 Repeat the layers, ending with the cake mixture. Arrange walnut halves on top. Bake in a preheated oven, 325°F/160°C, for 1–1^1/$_4$ hours, or until well risen and firm to the touch. Let cool in the pan for 10 minutes. Turn out, peel off the lining paper, and transfer to a wire rack to cool. Decorate with orange zest and serve in slices.

sponge cake

ingredients

MAKES 8–10 SLICES

6 oz/175 g butter, at room
temperature

6 oz/175 g/³/4 cup superfine
sugar

3 eggs, beaten

6 oz/175 g/scant 1¹/4 cups
self-rising flour

pinch of salt

3 tbsp raspberry jelly and
1 tbsp superfine or
confectioners' sugar,
to serve

method

1 Grease 2 x 8-inch/20-cm round sponge cake pans and base-line with parchment paper.

2 Beat the butter and sugar together in a mixing bowl using a wooden spoon or a hand-held mixer until the mixture is pale in color and light and fluffy. Add the egg, a little at a time, beating well after each addition.

3 Sift the flour and salt and carefully add to the mixture, folding it in with a metal spoon or a spatula. Divide the mixture among the pans and smooth over with the spatula. Place them on the same shelf in the center of a preheated oven, 350°F/180°C, and bake for 25–30 minutes until well risen, golden brown and beginning to shrink from the sides of the pan.

4 Remove from the oven and let stand for 1 minute. Loosen the cakes from around the edge of the pans using a round-bladed knife. Turn the cakes out onto a clean dish towel, remove the paper and invert them onto a wire rack (this prevents the wire rack from marking the top of the cakes). When completely cool, sandwich together with the jelly and sprinkle with the sugar.

mocha layer cake

ingredients

SERVES 8

7 oz/200 g/generous
    1¹/4 cups self-rising flour
¹/4 tsp baking powder
4 tbsp unsweetened cocoa
3¹/2 oz/100 g/¹/2 cup
    superfine sugar
2 eggs
2 tbsp corn syrup
5 fl oz/150 ml/²/3 cup corn oil
5 fl oz/150 ml/²/3 cup milk
butter, for greasing

filling

1 tsp instant coffee
1 tbsp boiling water
10 fl oz/300 ml/1¹/4 cups
    heavy cream
2 tbsp confectioners' sugar

to decorate

1³/4 oz/50 g semisweet
    chocolate, grated
chocolate caraque
confectioners' sugar,
    for dusting

method

1 Sift the flour, baking powder, and cocoa into a large bowl, then stir in the sugar. Make a well in the center and stir in the eggs, syrup, corn oil, and milk. Beat with a wooden spoon, gradually mixing in the dry ingredients to make a smooth batter. Divide the mixture among 3 lightly greased 3 x 7-inch/18-cm cake pans.

2 Bake in a preheated oven, 350°F/180°C, for 35–45 minutes, or until springy to the touch. Let stand in the pans for 5 minutes, then turn out and let cool completely on a wire rack.

3 To make the filling, dissolve the instant coffee in the boiling water and place in a large bowl with the cream and confectioners' sugar. Whip until the cream is just holding its shape, then use half the cream to sandwich the 3 cakes together. Spread the remaining cream over the top and sides of the cake. Press the grated chocolate into the cream round the edge of the cake.

4 Transfer the cake to a serving plate. Lay the chocolate caraque over the top of the cake. Cut a few thin strips of parchment paper and place on top of the chocolate caraque. Dust lightly with confectioners' sugar, then carefully remove the paper and serve.

coffee caramel cake

ingredients

SERVES 8

6 oz/175 g butter, softened,
  plus extra for greasing
6 oz/175 g/scant 1 cup
  golden superfine sugar
3 eggs, beaten
8 oz/225 g/generous $1^{1}/_{2}$ cups
  self-rising flour, sifted
$3^{1}/_{2}$ fl oz/100 ml/scant $^{1}/_{2}$ cup
  strong black coffee
chocolate-covered coffee
  beans, to decorate

frosting

4 fl oz/125 ml/$^{1}/_{2}$ cup milk
$4^{1}/_{2}$ oz/125 g butter
3 tbsp golden superfine sugar
1 lb $4^{1}/_{2}$ oz/575 g/$5^{3}/_{4}$ cups
  confectioners' sugar

method

1 Grease and base-line 2 x 8-inch/20-cm sponge cake pans. Place the butter and sugar in a bowl and beat together until light and fluffy. Gradually beat in the eggs, then fold in the flour and coffee. Divide the batter among the prepared pans and bake in a preheated oven, 350°F/180°C, for 30 minutes, or until well risen and springy when pressed in the center. Let cool in the pans for 5 minutes, then turn out and peel off the lining paper. Transfer to wire racks to cool completely.

2 To make the frosting, place the milk and butter in a pan, set over low heat, and stir until the butter has melted. Remove the pan from the heat and set aside. Place the superfine sugar in a separate, heavy-bottom pan and set over low heat, stirring constantly, until the sugar dissolves and turns a golden caramel. Remove from the heat and stir in the warm milk mixture. Return to the heat and stir until the caramel dissolves.

3 Remove from the heat and gradually stir in the confectioners' sugar, beating until the frosting is a smooth spreading consistency. Join the cakes together with some of the frosting and spread the rest over the top and sides. Decorate with chocolate-covered coffee beans.

torta de cielo

ingredients

SERVES 4–6

8 oz/225g/1 cup unsalted
   butter, at room
   temperature, plus extra
   for greasing

6 oz/175 g/1$^1/_4$ cups whole
   almonds, in their skins

8 oz/225 g/1$^1/_4$ cups sugar

3 eggs, lightly beaten

1 tsp almond extract

1 tsp vanilla extract

9 tbsp all-purpose flour

pinch of salt

to decorate

confectioners' sugar,
   for dusting

slivered almonds, toasted

method

1 Lightly grease an 8-inch/20-cm round cake pan and line the pan with parchment paper.

2 Place the almonds in a food processor and process to form a "mealy" mixture. Set aside.

3 Beat the butter and sugar together in a large bowl until smooth and fluffy. Beat in the eggs, almonds, and both the almond and vanilla extracts until well blended. Stir in the flour and salt and mix briefly, until the flour is just incorporated.

4 Pour or spoon the batter into the prepared pan and smooth the surface. Bake in a preheated oven, 350°F/180°C, for 40–50 minutes, or until the cake feels spongy when gently pressed.

5 Remove from the oven and let stand on a wire rack to cool. To serve, dust with confectioners' sugar and decorate with toasted slivered almonds.

chocolate truffle torte

ingredients

SERVES 10

butter, for greasing

2 oz/55 g/generous $^1/_4$ cup golden superfine sugar

2 eggs

1 oz/25 g/scant $^1/_4$ cup all-purpose flour

1 oz/25 g/$^1/_4$ cup unsweetened cocoa, plus extra to decorate

2 fl oz/50 ml/$^1/_4$ cup cold strong black coffee

2 tbsp brandy

topping

20 fl oz/600 ml/2$^1/_2$ cups heavy cream

15 oz/425 g semisweet chocolate, melted and cooled

confectioners' sugar, to decorate

method

1 Grease a 9-inch/23-cm springform cake pan with butter and line the bottom with parchment paper. Place the sugar and eggs in a heatproof bowl and set over a pan of hot water. Whisk together until pale and mousse-like. Sift the flour and unsweetened cocoa into a separate bowl, then fold gently into the cake batter. Pour into the prepared pan and bake in a preheated oven, 425°F/220°C, for 7–10 minutes, or until risen and firm to the touch.

2 Transfer to a wire rack to cool. Wash and dry the pan and put the cooled cake back in the pan. Mix the coffee and brandy together and brush over the cake.

3 To make the topping, place the cream in a bowl and whip until very soft peaks form. Carefully fold in the cooled chocolate. Pour the chocolate mixture over the sponge and let chill in the refrigerator for 4–5 hours, or until set.

4 To decorate the torte, sift unsweetened cocoa over the top and remove carefully from the pan. Using strips of card or waxed paper, sift bands of confectioners' sugar over the torte to create a striped pattern. To serve, cut into slices with a hot knife.

almond & hazelnut gateau

ingredients

SERVES 8

4 eggs

3¹/₂ oz/100 g/¹/₂ cup
   superfine sugar

1³/₄ oz/50 g/¹/₂ cup
   ground almonds

1³/₄ oz/50 g/¹/₂ cup
   ground hazelnuts

5¹/₂ tbsp all-purpose flour

butter, for greasing

1³/₄ oz/50 g/scant ¹/₂ cup
   slivered almonds

confectioners' sugar,
   for dusting

filling

3¹/₂ oz/100 g semisweet
   chocolate

1 tbsp butter

10 fl oz/300 ml/1¹/₄ cups
   heavy cream

method

1 Whisk the eggs and superfine sugar together for 10 minutes, or until light and foamy and the whisk leaves a trail that lasts a few seconds when lifted. Fold in the ground almonds and hazelnuts, sift the flour and fold in with a metal spoon or spatula. Pour into 2 lightly greased and base-lined 7-inch/18-cm round sandwich cake pans.

2 Sprinkle the slivered almonds over the top of one of the cakes, then bake both cakes in a preheated oven, 375°F/190°C, for 15–20 minutes, or until springy to the touch. Let cool in the pans for 5 minutes, then turn out onto wire racks to cool completely.

3 To make the filling, melt the chocolate, remove from the heat, and stir in the butter. Let cool. Whip the cream until holding its shape, then fold in the chocolate until mixed.

4 Place the cake without extra almonds on a serving plate and spread the filling over it. Let set slightly, then place the almond-topped cake on top of the filling and let chill in the refrigerator for 1 hour. Dust with confectioners' sugar and serve.

moroccan orange & almond cake

ingredients

SERVES 8

1 orange
4 oz/115 g butter, softened,
    plus extra for greasing
4 oz/115 g/generous 1/2 cup
    golden superfine sugar
2 eggs, beaten
6 oz/175 g/scant 1 cup
    semolina
3 1/2 oz/100 g/generous 1 cup
    ground almonds
1 1/2 tsp baking powder
confectioners' sugar, for
    dusting
strained plain yogurt, to serve

syrup

10 fl oz/300 ml/1 1/4 cups
    orange juice
4 3/4 oz/130 g/2/3 cup
    superfine sugar
8 cardamom pods, crushed

method

1 Grate the rind from the orange, reserving some for the decoration, and squeeze the juice from one half. Place the butter, orange rind, and sugar in a bowl and beat together until light and fluffy. Gradually beat in the eggs.

2 In a separate bowl, mix the semolina, ground almonds, and baking powder, then fold into the creamed mixture with the orange juice. Spoon the batter into a greased and base-lined 8-inch/20-cm cake pan and bake in a preheated oven, 350°F/180°C, for 30–40 minutes, or until well risen and a skewer inserted into the center comes out clean. Let cool in the pan for 10 minutes.

3 To make the syrup, place the orange juice, sugar, and cardamom pods in a pan over low heat and stir until the sugar has dissolved. Bring to a boil and let simmer for 4 minutes, or until syrupy.

4 Turn the cake out into a deep serving dish. Using a skewer, make holes over the surface of the warm cake. Strain the syrup into a separate bowl and spoon three-fourths of it over the cake, then let stand for 30 minutes. Dust the cake with confectioners' sugar and cut into slices. Serve with the remaining syrup drizzled around, accompanied by strained plain yogurt decorated with the reserved orange rind.

german chocolate & hazelnut cake

ingredients

SERVES 8

6 oz/175 g unsalted butter,
softened, plus extra
for greasing

4 oz/115 g/³/₄ cup dark brown
sugar

6 oz/175 g/scant 1 cup self-
rising flour, plus extra
for dusting

1 tbsp unsweetened cocoa

1 tsp allspice

3 eggs, beaten

4 oz/115 g/1 cup ground
hazelnuts

2 tbsp black coffee

confectioners' sugar, for dusting

method

1 Grease and flour a 7¹/₂-inch/19-cm kugelhopf pan. Place the butter and brown sugar in a large mixing bowl and beat together until light and fluffy. Sift the self-rising flour, unsweetened cocoa, and allspice into a separate bowl.

2 Beat the eggs into the creamed batter, one at a time, adding 1 tablespoon of the flour mixture with the second and third eggs. Fold in the remaining flour mixture, ground hazelnuts, and coffee.

3 Turn into the prepared pan and bake in a preheated oven, 350°F/180°C, for 45–50 minutes, or until the cake springs back when lightly pressed. Let stand in the pan for 10 minutes, then turn out onto a wire rack to cool completely. Dust generously with confectioners' sugar before serving.

caribbean coconut cake

ingredients

SERVES 8

10 oz/280 g butter, softened,
    plus extra for greasing

6 oz/175 g/scant 1 cup
    golden superfine sugar

3 eggs

6 oz/175 g/1¼ cups self-
    rising flour

1½ tsp baking powder

½ tsp freshly grated nutmeg

2 oz/55 g/⅔ cup dry
    unsweetened coconut

5 tbsp coconut cream

10 oz/280 g/2¾ cups
    confectioners' sugar

5 tbsp pineapple jelly

dry unsweetened coconut,
    toasted, to decorate

method

1 Grease and base-line 2 x 8-inch/20-cm sponge cake pans. Place 6 oz/175 g of the butter in a bowl with the sugar and eggs and sift in the flour, baking powder, and nutmeg. Beat together until smooth, then stir in the coconut and 2 tablespoons of the coconut cream into the mixture.

2 Divide the mixture among the prepared pans and smooth the tops. Bake in a preheated oven, 350°F/180°C, for 25 minutes, or until golden and firm to the touch. Let cool in the pans for 5 minutes, then turn out onto a wire rack, peel off the lining paper, and let cool completely.

3 Sift the confectioners' sugar into a bowl and add the remaining butter and coconut cream. Beat together until smooth. Spread the pineapple jelly on one of the cakes and top with just under half of the buttercream. Place the other cake on top. Spread the remaining buttercream on top of the cake and scatter with the toasted coconut.

honey spiced cake

ingredients

SERVES 8

5^1/2 oz/150 g butter, plus
   extra for greasing

4 oz/115 g/generous ^{1}/2 cup
   brown sugar

6 oz/175 g/^{1}/2 cup honey

1 tbsp water

7 oz/200 g/scant 1^1/2 cups
   self-rising flour

^{1}/2 tsp ground ginger

^{1}/2 tsp ground cinnamon

^{1}/2 tsp caraway seeds

seeds from 8 cardamom pods,
   ground

2 eggs, beaten

12 oz/350 g/3^1/2 cups
   confectioners' sugar

method

1 Grease a 28-fl oz/875-ml/3^1/2-cup fluted cake pan. Place the butter, sugar, honey, and water into a heavy-bottom pan. Set over low heat and stir until the butter has melted and the sugar has dissolved. Remove from the heat and let cool for 10 minutes.

2 Sift the flour into a bowl and mix in the ginger, cinnamon, caraway seeds, and cardamom. Make a well in the center. Pour in the honey mixture and the eggs and beat well until smooth. Pour the batter into the prepared pan and bake in a preheated oven, 350°F/ 180°C, for 40–50 minutes, or until well risen and a skewer inserted into the center comes out clean. Let cool in the pan for 5 minutes, then transfer to a wire rack to cool completely.

3 Sift the confectioners' sugar into a bowl. Stir in enough warm water to make a smooth, flowing frosting. Spoon over the cake, allowing it to flow down the sides, then let set.

rich chocolate cake

ingredients

MAKES 10–12 SLICES

3$\frac{1}{2}$ oz/100 g/generous
$\frac{1}{2}$ cup raisins

finely grated rind and juice
of 1 orange

6 oz/175 g butter, diced, plus
extra for greasing the pan

3$\frac{1}{2}$ oz/100 g semisweet
chocolate, at least
70% cocoa solids,
broken up

4 large eggs, beaten

3$\frac{1}{2}$ oz/100 g/$\frac{1}{2}$ cup
superfine sugar

1 tsp vanilla extract

2 oz/55 g/scant $\frac{1}{2}$ cup
all-purpose flour

2 oz/55 g/generous $\frac{1}{2}$ cup
ground almonds

$\frac{1}{2}$ tsp baking powder

pinch salt

2 oz/55g/scant $\frac{1}{2}$ cup
blanched almonds,
toasted and chopped

confectioners' sugar, sifted,
to decorate

method

1 Put the raisins in a small bowl, add the orange juice, and let soak for 20 minutes. Line a deep 10-inch/25-cm round cake pan with a removable bottom with waxed paper and grease the paper; set aside.

2 Melt the butter and chocolate together in a small pan over medium heat, stirring. Remove from the heat and set aside to cool.

3 Using an electric mixer beat the eggs, sugar, and vanilla together for about 3 minutes until light and fluffy. Stir in the cooled chocolate mixture.

4 Drain the raisins if they haven't absorbed all the orange juice. Sift over the flour, ground almonds, baking powder, and salt. Add the raisins, orange rind, and almonds, and fold everything together.

5 Spoon into the cake pan and smooth the surface. Bake in a preheated oven, 350°F/ 180°C, for about 40 minutes, or until a toothpick inserted into the center comes out clean and the cake starts to come away from the side of the pan. Let cool in the pan for 10 minutes, then remove from the pan and let cool completely on a wire rack. Dust with confectioners' sugar before serving.

rich fruit cake

ingredients

SERVES 4

butter, for greasing

6 oz/175 g/1 cup pitted
   unsweetened dates

4^1/$_2$ oz/125 g/^{3}/$_4$ cup no-soak
   dried prunes

7 fl oz/200 ml/scant 1 cup
   unsweetened orange juice

2 tbsp molasses

1 tsp finely grated lemon rind

1 tsp finely grated orange rind

8 oz/225 g/generous 1^1/$_2$ cups
   whole-wheat self-rising flour

1 tsp pumpkin pie spice

4^1/$_2$ oz/125 g/^{3}/$_4$ cup seedless
   raisins

4^1/$_2$ oz/125 g/^{3}/$_4$ cup golden
   raisins

4^1/$_2$ oz/125 g/generous ^{3}/$_4$ cup
   currants

4^1/$_2$ oz/125 g/^{3}/$_4$ cup dried
   cranberries

3 large eggs, separated

1 tbsp apricot jelly, warmed

frosting

4^1/$_2$ oz/125 g/generous 1 cup
   confectioners' sugar, plus
   extra for dusting

1–2 tsp water

1 tsp vanilla extract

orange and lemon rind strips,
   to decorate

method

1 Grease and line a deep 8-inch/20-cm round cake pan. Chop the dates and prunes and place in a pan. Pour over the orange juice and let simmer for 10 minutes. Remove the pan from the heat and beat the fruit mixture until puréed. Add the molasses and citrus rinds and let cool.

2 Sift the flour and spice into a bowl, adding any bran that remains in the strainer. Add the dried fruits. When the date and prune mixture is cool, whisk in the egg yolks. Whisk the egg whites in a separate, clean bowl until stiff. Spoon the fruit mixture into the dry ingredients and mix together.

3 Gently fold in the egg whites. Transfer to the prepared pan and bake in a preheated oven, 325°F/160°C, for 1^1/$_2$ hours. Let cool in the pan.

4 Remove the cake from the pan and brush the top with jelly. To make the frosting, sift the sugar into a bowl and mix with enough water and the vanilla extract to form a soft frosting. Lay the frosting over the top of the cake and trim the edges. Decorate with orange and lemon rind.

chocolate cherry gateau

ingredients

**MAKES ONE 9-INCH/
23-CM CAKE**

3 tbsp unsalted butter, melted,
    plus extra for greasing
2 lb/900 g fresh cherries,
    pitted and halved
9 oz/250 g/generous 1¼ cups
    superfine sugar
3½ fl oz/100 ml/scant ½ cup
    cherry brandy
3½ oz/100 g/¾ cup all-
    purpose flour
1¾ oz/50 g/½ cup
    unsweetened cocoa
½ tsp baking powder
4 eggs
32 fl oz/1 liter/4 cups heavy
    cream
grated semisweet chocolate
whole fresh cherries,
    to decorate

method

1 Grease and line a 9-inch/23-cm springform cake pan. Put the halved cherries into a pan, and add 3 tablespoons of the sugar and the cherry brandy. Simmer for 5 minutes. Strain, reserving the syrup. In another bowl, sift together the flour, cocoa, and baking powder.

2 Put the eggs in a heatproof bowl and beat in 5¾ oz/160 g/generous ¾ cup of the sugar. Place the bowl over a pan of simmering water and beat for 6 minutes until thickened. Remove from the heat, then gradually fold in the flour mixture and melted butter. Spoon into the cake pan. Bake in a preheated oven, 350°F/180°C, for 40 minutes. Remove from the oven and let cool.

3 Turn out the cake and cut in half horizontally. Mix the cream with the remaining sugar. Spread the reserved syrup over the cut sides of the cake. Arrange the cherries over one half, top with a layer of cream, and place the other half on top. Cover with cream, press grated chocolate all over, and decorate with cherries.

blueberry & lemon drizzle cake

ingredients

SERVES 12

8 oz/225 g butter, softened,
    plus extra for greasing
8 oz/225 g/generous 1 cup
    golden superfine sugar
4 eggs, beaten
9 oz/250 g/1$^{3}/_{4}$ cups self-rising
    flour, sifted
finely grated rind and juice
    of 1 lemon
1 oz/25 g/generous $^{1}/_{4}$ cup
    ground almonds
7 oz/200 g fresh blueberries

topping

juice of 2 lemons
4 oz/115 g/generous $^{1}/_{2}$ cup
    golden superfine sugar

method

1 Grease and line the bottom of an 8-inch/ 20-cm square cake pan. Place the butter and sugar in a bowl and beat together until light and fluffy. Gradually beat in the eggs, adding a little flour toward the end to prevent curdling. Beat in the lemon rind, then fold in the remaining flour and almonds with enough of the lemon juice to give a good dropping consistency.

2 Fold in three-fourths of the blueberries and turn into the prepared pan. Smooth the surface, then scatter the remaining blueberries on top. Bake in a preheated oven, 350°F/180°C, for 1 hour, or until firm to the touch and a skewer inserted into the center comes out clean.

3 To make the topping, place the lemon juice and sugar in a bowl and mix together. As soon as the cake comes out of the oven, prick it all over with a fine skewer and pour over the lemon mixture. Let cool in the pan until completely cold, then cut into 12 squares to serve.

apple streusel cake

ingredients

SERVES 8

4 oz/115 g butter, plus extra
    for greasing

1 lb/450 g tart cooking apples

6 oz/175 g/1$^1/4$ cups self-
    rising flour

1 tsp ground cinnamon

pinch of salt

4 oz/115 g/generous $^1/2$ cup
    golden superfine sugar

2 eggs

1–2 tbsp milk

confectioners' sugar,
    for dusting

streusel topping

4 oz/115 g/generous $^3/4$ cup
    self-rising flour

6 tbsp butter

3 oz/85 g/scant $^1/2$ cup
    golden superfine sugar

method

1 Grease a 9-inch/23-cm springform cake pan. To make the streusel topping, sift the flour into a bowl and rub in the butter until the mixture resembles coarse crumbs. Stir in the sugar and set aside.

2 Peel, core, and thinly slice the apples. To make the cake, sift the flour into a bowl with the cinnamon and salt. Place the butter and sugar in a separate bowl and beat together until light and fluffy. Gradually beat in the eggs, adding a little of the flour mixture with the last addition of egg. Gently fold in half the remaining flour mixture, then fold in the rest with the milk.

3 Spoon the batter into the prepared pan and smooth the top. Cover with the sliced apples and sprinkle the streusel topping evenly over the top. Bake in a preheated oven, 350°F/180°C, for 1 hour, or until browned and firm to the touch. Let cool in the pan before removing the side. Dust the cake with confectioners' sugar before serving.

banana & lime cake

ingredients

SERVES 10

butter, for greasing

10¹/₂ oz/300 g/scant 2 cups
   all-purpose flour

1 tsp salt

1¹/₂ tsp baking powder

6 oz/175 g/scant ⁷/₈ cup
   firmly packed brown sugar

1 tsp grated lime rind

1 egg, beaten

1 banana, mashed with
   1 tbsp lime juice

5 fl oz/150 ml/²/₃ cup lowfat
   cream cheese

4 oz/115 g/²/₃ cup golden
   raisins

topping

4 oz/115 g/1 cup
   confectioners' sugar

1–2 tsp lime juice

¹/₂ tsp finely grated lime rind

to decorate

banana chips

finely grated lime rind

method

1 Grease and line a deep 7-inch/18-cm round cake pan with parchment paper. Sift the flour, salt, and baking powder into a large bowl and stir in the sugar and lime rind.

2 Make a well in the center of the dry ingredients and add the egg, banana, cream cheese, and golden raisins. Mix well until thoroughly incorporated. Spoon the batter into the pan and smooth the surface.

3 Bake in a preheated oven, 350°F/180°C, for 40–45 minutes, or until firm to the touch or until a skewer inserted in the center comes out clean. Let the cake cool in the pan for 10 minutes, then turn out onto a wire rack to cool completely.

4 To make the topping, sift the confectioners' sugar into a small bowl and mix with the lime juice to form a soft, but not too runny frosting. Stir in the grated lime rind. Drizzle the frosting over the cake, letting it run down the sides. Decorate the cake with banana chips and lime rind. Let the cake stand for 15 minutes so that the frosting sets.

pear & ginger cake

ingredients

SERVES 6

7 oz/200 g/scant 1 cup
  unsalted butter, softened,
  plus extra for greasing
6 oz/175 g/generous ³/4 cup
  superfine sugar
6 oz/175 g/1¹/4 cups self-
  rising flour, sifted
1 tbsp ground ginger
3 eggs, beaten lightly
1 lb/450 g pears, peeled, cored,
  and thinly sliced, then
  brushed with lemon juice
1 tbsp brown sugar
ice cream or heavy cream,
  lightly whipped, to serve
  (optional)

method

1 Lightly grease a deep 8-inch/20-cm cake pan with butter and line the bottom with baking parchment.

2 Mix all but 2 tablespoons of the butter with the superfine sugar, flour, ginger, and eggs in a bowl. Beat with a whisk until the mixture forms a smooth consistency.

3 Spoon the cake batter into the prepared pan and level out the surface with a spatula. Arrange the pear slices over the cake batter. Sprinkle with the brown sugar and dot with the remaining butter.

4 Bake in a preheated oven, 350°F/180°C, for 35–40 minutes, or until the cake is golden on top and feels springy to the touch. Serve warm, with ice cream or whipped cream, if you like.

small
bites

Small bites—muffins, cupcakes, cookies, and bars—have a very special appeal, perhaps because they have a delightfully self-indulgent, 'just for me' feel about them!

Children love small bites, so they'll be thrilled to find a treat in their school lunchbag—a Drizzled Honey Cupcake, Apple & Cinnamon Muffin, Spiced Chocolate Muffin, Fruit & Nut Square, or an Oat & Hazelnut Morsel or two will revive them after the morning's exertions and set them up for the afternoon. When they get home from school, let them get their fingers sticky with a Frosted Peanut Butter Cupcake, Sticky Gingerbread Cupcake, Banana & Pecan Cupcake, or a Lemon Butterfly Cake—gorgeously messy!

Grown-ups—probably as an antidote to being grown up—love anything with a hint of wickedness and preferably more than a hint of chocolate! Devil's Food Cakes with Chocolate Frosting, Chocolate Temptations, and Warm Molten-centered Chocolate Cupcakes are satisfyingly naughty.

For more sedate adult occasions, Fudge Nut Muffins, Fig & Almond Muffins, Lavender Cookies, and Fig & Walnut Cookies are simply delicious, and a Rose Petal Cupcake, with its delicate pink frosting, is a thoughtful treat to serve on a birthday or anniversary.

drizzled honey cupcakes

ingredients

MAKES 12

3 oz/85 g/generous $^{1}/_{2}$ cup
   self-rising flour
$^{1}/_{4}$ tsp ground cinnamon
pinch of ground cloves
pinch of grated nutmeg
6 tbsp butter, softened
3 oz/85 g/scant $^{1}/_{2}$ cup
   superfine sugar
1 tbsp honey
finely grated rind of 1 orange
2 eggs, lightly beaten
$1^{1}/_{2}$ oz/40 g/$^{3}/_{4}$ cup walnut
   pieces, minced

topping

$^{1}/_{2}$ oz/15 g/$^{1}/_{8}$ cup walnut
   pieces, minced
$^{1}/_{4}$ tsp ground cinnamon
2 tbsp honey
juice of 1 orange

method

1 Put 12 paper baking cases in a muffin pan, or place 12 double-layer paper cases on a cookie sheet.

2 Sift the flour, cinnamon, cloves, and nutmeg together into a bowl. Put the butter and sugar in a separate bowl and beat together until light and fluffy. Beat in the honey and orange rind, then gradually add the eggs, beating well after each addition. Using a metal spoon, fold in the flour mixture. Stir in the walnuts, then spoon the batter into the paper cases.

3 Bake the cupcakes in a preheated oven, 375°F/190°C, for 20 minutes, or until well risen and golden brown. Transfer to a wire rack and let cool.

4 To make the topping, mix together the walnuts and cinnamon. Put the honey and orange juice in a pan and heat gently, stirring, until combined.

5 When the cupcakes have almost cooled, prick the tops all over with a fork or skewer and then drizzle with the warm honey mixture. Sprinkle the walnut mixture over the top of each cupcake and serve warm or cold.

frosted peanut butter cupcakes

ingredients

MAKES 16

4 tbsp butter, softened,
   or soft margarine
8 oz/225 g/scant 1^1/$_4$ cups
   firmly packed brown sugar
4 oz/115 g/generous ^{1}/$_3$ cup
   crunchy peanut butter
2 eggs, lightly beaten
1 tsp vanilla extract
8 oz/225 g/generous
   1^1/$_2$ cups all-purpose flour
2 tsp baking powder
3^1/$_2$ fl oz/100 ml/generous
   ^{1}/$_3$ cup milk

frosting

7 oz/200 g/scant 1 cup
   full-fat soft cream cheese
2 tbsp butter, softened
8 oz/225 g/2 cups
   confectioners' sugar

method

1 Put 16 muffin paper cases in a muffin pan.

2 Put the butter, sugar, and peanut butter in a bowl and beat together for 1–2 minutes, or until well mixed. Gradually add the eggs, beating well after each addition, then add the vanilla extract. Sift in the flour and baking powder and then, using a metal spoon, fold them into the mixture, alternating with the milk. Spoon the batter into the paper cases.

3 Bake the cupcakes in a preheated oven, 350°F/180°C, for 25 minutes, or until well risen and golden brown. Transfer to a wire rack and let cool.

4 To make the frosting, put the cream cheese and butter in a large bowl and, using an electric hand whisk, beat together until smooth. Sift the confectioners' sugar into the mixture, then beat together until well mixed.

5 When the cupcakes are cold, spread the frosting on top of each cupcake, swirling it with a round-bladed knife. Store the cupcakes in the refrigerator until ready to serve.

rose petal cupcakes

ingredients

MAKES 12

8 tbsp butter, softened

4 oz/115 g/generous $\frac{1}{2}$ cup
    superfine sugar

2 eggs, lightly beaten

1 tbsp milk

few drops of extract of rose oil

$\frac{1}{4}$ tsp vanilla extract

6 oz/175 g/scant $1\frac{1}{4}$ cups
    self-rising white flour

silver dragées (cake decoration
    balls), to decorate

frosting

6 tbsp butter, softened

6 oz/175 g/$1\frac{1}{2}$ cups
    confectioners' sugar

pink or purple food coloring
    (optional)

candied
rose petals

12–24 rose petals

lightly beaten egg white,
    for brushing

superfine sugar, for sprinkling

method

1 To make the candied rose petals, gently rinse the petals and dry well with paper towels. Carefully brush both sides of a rose petal with egg white, then coat well with superfine sugar. Place on a tray and repeat with the remaining petals. Cover the tray with foil and let dry overnight.

2 Put 12 paper baking cases in a muffin pan, or place 12 double-layer paper cases on a cookie sheet.

3 Put the butter and sugar in a bowl and beat together until light and fluffy. Gradually add the eggs, beating well after each addition. Stir in the milk, rose oil extract, and vanilla extract then, using a metal spoon, fold in the flour. Spoon the batter into the paper cases.

4 Bake the cupcakes in a preheated oven, 400°F/200°C, for 12–15 minutes, or until well risen and golden brown. Transfer to a wire rack and let cool.

5 To make the frosting, put the butter in a large bowl and beat until fluffy. Sift in the confectioners' sugar and mix well together. If wished, add a few drops of pink or purple food coloring to complement the rose petals.

6 When the cupcakes are cold, spread the frosting on top of each cake. Top with 1–2 candied rose petals and sprinkle with silver dragées to decorate.

sticky gingerbread cupcakes

ingredients

MAKES 16

4 oz/115 g/generous ³/₄ cup
   all-purpose flour
2 tsp ground ginger
³/₄ tsp ground cinnamon
1 piece of preserved
   ginger, minced
³/₄ tsp baking soda
4 tbsp milk
6 tbsp butter, softened,
   or soft margarine
2¹/₂ oz/70 g/generous ¹/₃ cup
   firmly packed brown sugar
2 tbsp molasses
2 eggs, lightly beaten
pieces of preserved ginger,
   to decorate

frosting

6 tbsp butter, softened
6 oz/175 g/1¹/₂ cups
   confectioners' sugar
2 tbsp ginger syrup from the
   preserved ginger jar

method

1 Put 16 paper baking cases in a muffin pan, or place 16 double-layer paper cases on a cookie sheet.

2 Sift the flour, ground ginger, and cinnamon together into a bowl. Add the minced ginger and toss in the flour mixture until well coated. In a separate bowl, dissolve the baking soda in the milk.

3 Put the butter and sugar in a bowl and beat together until fluffy. Beat in the molasses, then gradually add the eggs, beating well after each addition. Beat in the flour mixture, then gradually beat in the milk. Spoon the batter into the paper cases.

4 Bake the cupcakes in a preheated oven, 325°F/160°C, for 20 minutes, or until well risen and golden brown. Transfer to a wire rack and let cool.

5 To make the frosting, put the butter in a bowl and beat until fluffy. Sift in the sugar, add the ginger syrup, and beat together until smooth and creamy. Slice the preserved ginger into thin slivers or chop finely.

6 When the cupcakes are cold, spread the frosting on top of each cupcake, then decorate with pieces of ginger.

fudge nut muffins

ingredients

MAKES 12

9 oz/250 g/generous
   1³/4 cups all-purpose flour
4 tsp baking powder
3 oz/85 g/scant ¹/2 cup
   superfine sugar
6 tbsp crunchy peanut butter
1 large egg, beaten
4 tbsp butter, melted
6 fl oz/175 ml/³/4 cup milk
5¹/2 oz/150 g vanilla fudge,
   cut into small pieces
3 tbsp coarsely chopped
   unsalted peanuts

method

1 Line a 12-cup muffin pan with double muffin paper liners. Sift the flour and baking powder into a bowl. Stir in the superfine sugar. Add the peanut butter and stir until the mixture resembles bread crumbs.

2 Place the egg, butter, and milk in a separate bowl and beat until blended, then stir into the dry ingredients until just blended. Lightly stir in the fudge pieces. Divide the batter evenly among the muffin liners.

3 Sprinkle the chopped peanuts on top and bake in a preheated oven, 400°F/200°C, for 20–25 minutes until well risen and firm to the touch. Remove the muffins from the oven and let cool for 2 minutes, then place them on a cooling rack and let cool completely.

fig & almond muffins

ingredients

MAKES 12

2 tbsp sunflower or peanut
   oil, plus extra for oiling
   (if using)
9 oz/250 g/generous
   1³/₄ cups all purpose flour
1 tsp baking soda
¹/₂ tsp salt
8 oz/225 g/1 cup raw sugar
3 oz/85 g/generous ¹/₂ cup
   dried figs, chopped
4 oz/115 g/1 cup almonds,
   chopped
8 fl oz/250 ml/1 cup water
1 tsp almond extract
2 tbsp chopped almonds,
   to decorate

method

1 Oil a 12-cup muffin pan with sunflower oil, or line it with 12 muffin paper liners. Sift the flour, baking soda, and salt into a mixing bowl. Then add the raw sugar and stir together.

2 In a separate bowl, mix the figs, almonds, and remaining sunflower oil together. Then stir in the water and almond extract. Add the fruit and nut mixture to the flour mixture and gently stir together. Do not overstir—it is fine for it to be a little lumpy.

3 Divide the muffin batter evenly among the 12 cups in the muffin pan or the paper liners (they should be about two-thirds full), then sprinkle over the remaining chopped almonds to decorate. Transfer to a preheated oven, 375°F/190°C, and bake for 25 minutes, or until risen and golden.

4 Remove the muffins from the oven and serve warm, or place them on a cooling rack and let cool.

banana & pecan cupcakes

ingredients

MAKES 12

8 oz/225 g/generous
  1^1/$_2$ cups all-purpose flour

1^1/$_4$ tsp baking powder

^{1}/$_4$ tsp baking soda

2 ripe bananas

8 tbsp butter, softened,
  or soft margarine

4 oz/115 g/generous ^{1}/$_2$ cup
  superfine sugar

^{1}/$_2$ tsp vanilla extract

2 eggs, lightly beaten

4 tbsp sour cream

2 oz/55 g/^{1}/$_2$ cup pecans,
  coarsely chopped

topping

8 tbsp butter, softened

4 oz/115 g/1 cup
  confectioners' sugar

1 oz/25 g/^{1}/$_4$ cup pecans,
  minced

method

1 Put 24 paper baking cases in a muffin pan, or place 24 double-layer paper cases on a cookie sheet.

2 Sift together the flour, baking powder, and baking soda. Peel the bananas, put them in a bowl, and mash with a fork.

3 Put the butter, sugar, and vanilla in a bowl and beat together until light and fluffy. Gradually add the eggs, beating well after each addition. Stir in the mashed bananas and sour cream. Using a metal spoon, fold in the sifted flour mixture and chopped nuts, then spoon the batter into the paper cases.

4 Bake the cupcakes in a preheated oven, 375°F/190°C, for 20 minutes, or until well risen and golden brown. Transfer to a wire rack and let cool.

5 To make the topping, beat the butter in a bowl until fluffy. Sift in the confectioners' sugar and mix together well. Spread the frosting on top of each cupcake and sprinkle with the minced pecans before serving.

apple & cinnamon muffins

ingredients

MAKES 6

3 oz/85 g/scant $^2/_3$ cup all-
    purpose whole wheat flour
2$^1/_2$ oz/70 g/$^1/_2$ cup all-
    purpose white flour
1$^1/_2$ tsp baking powder
pinch of salt
1 tsp ground cinnamon
1$^1/_2$ oz/40 g/scant $^1/_4$ cup
    golden superfine sugar
2 small eating apples, peeled,
    cored, and finely chopped
4 fl oz/125 ml/$^1/_2$ cup milk
1 egg, beaten
4 tbsp butter, melted

topping

12 brown sugar lumps,
    coarsely crushed
$^1/_2$ tsp ground cinnamon

method

1 Place 6 muffin paper liners in a muffin pan.

2 Sift both flours, baking powder, salt, and cinnamon together into a large bowl and stir in the sugar and chopped apples. Place the milk, egg, and butter in a separate bowl and mix. Add the wet ingredients to the dry ingredients and gently stir until just combined.

3 Divide the batter evenly among the paper liners. To make the topping, mix the crushed sugar lumps and cinnamon together and sprinkle over the muffins. Bake in a preheated oven, 400°F/ 200°C, for 20–25 minutes, or until risen and golden. Remove the muffins from the oven and serve warm or place them on a cooling rack and let cool.

moist walnut cupcakes

ingredients

MAKES 12

3 oz/85 g/³/₄ cup walnuts

4 tbsp butter, softened

3¹/₂ oz/100 g/¹/₂ cup
    superfine sugar

grated rind of ¹/₂ lemon

2¹/₂ oz/70 g/¹/₂ cup
    self-rising white flour

2 eggs

12 walnut halves, to decorate

frosting

4 tbsp butter, softened

3 oz/85 g/³/₄ cup
    confectioners' sugar

grated rind of ¹/₂ lemon

1 tsp lemon juice

method

1 Put 12 paper baking cases in a muffin pan, or place 12 double-layer paper cases on a cookie sheet.

2 Put the walnuts in a food processor and, using a pulsating action, blend until finely ground, being careful not to overgrind, which will turn them to oil. Add the butter, cut into small pieces, along with the sugar, lemon rind, flour, and eggs, then blend until evenly mixed. Spoon the batter into the paper cases.

3 Bake the cupcakes in a preheated oven, 375°F/190°C, for 20 minutes, or until well risen and golden brown. Transfer to a wire rack and let cool.

4 To make the frosting, put the butter in a bowl and beat until fluffy. Sift in the confectioners' sugar, add the lemon rind and juice, and mix well together.

5 When the cupcakes are cold, spread the frosting on top of each cupcake and top with a walnut to decorate.

walnut & cinnamon blondies

ingredients

MAKES 9 SQUARES

4 oz/115 g butter, plus extra
    for greasing
8 oz/225 g/generous 1 cup
    brown sugar
1 egg
1 egg yolk
5 oz/150 g/1 cup
    self-rising flour
1 tsp ground cinnamon
3 oz/85 g/generous 1/2 cup
    coarsely chopped walnuts

method

1 Place the butter and sugar in a pan over low heat and stir until the sugar has dissolved. Cook, stirring, for an additional 1 minute. The mixture will bubble slightly, but do not let it boil. Let cool for 10 minutes.

2 Stir the egg and egg yolk into the mixture. Sift in the flour and cinnamon, add the nuts, and stir until just blended. Pour the cake batter into a greased and base-lined 7-inch/18-cm square cake pan, then bake in a preheated oven, 350°F/180°C, for 20–25 minutes, or until springy in the center and a skewer inserted into the center of the cake comes out clean.

3 Let cool in the pan for a few minutes, then run a knife round the edge of the cake to loosen it. Turn the cake out onto a wire rack and peel off the paper. Let cool completely. When cold, cut into squares.

lemon butterfly cakes

ingredients

MAKES 12

4 oz/115 g/generous ³/₄ cup
   self-rising flour

¹/₂ tsp baking powder

8 tbsp soft margarine

4 oz/115 g/generous ¹/₂ cup
   superfine sugar

2 eggs, lightly beaten

finely grated rind of ¹/₂ lemon

2 tbsp milk

confectioners' sugar,
   for dusting

lemon filling

6 tbsp butter, softened

6 oz/175 g/1¹/₂ cups
   confectioners' sugar, plus
   extra for dusting

1 tbsp lemon juice

method

1 Put 12 paper baking cases in a muffin pan, or place 12 double-layer paper cases on a cookie sheet.

2 Sift the flour and baking powder into a large bowl. Add the margarine, sugar, eggs, lemon rind, and milk and, using an electric hand whisk, beat together until smooth. Spoon the batter into the paper cases.

3 Bake the cupcakes in a preheated oven, 375°F/190°C, for 15–20 minutes, or until well risen and golden brown. Transfer to a wire rack and let cool.

4 To make the filling, put the butter in a bowl and beat until fluffy. Sift in the confectioners' sugar, add the lemon juice, and beat together until smooth and creamy.

5 When the cupcakes are cold, use a serrated knife to cut a circle from the top of each cupcake and then cut each circle in half. Spread or pipe a little of the buttercream filling into the center of each cupcake, then press the 2 semicircular halves into it at an angle, to resemble butterfly wings. Dust with sifted confectioners' sugar before serving.

warm molten-centered chocolate cupcakes

ingredients

MAKES 8

4 tbsp soft margarine

2 oz/55 g/generous $^1/_4$ cup
    superfine sugar

1 large egg

3 oz/85 g/generous $^1/_2$ cup
    self-rising flour

1 tbsp unsweetened cocoa

2 oz/55 g semisweet
    chocolate

confectioners' sugar,
    for dusting

method

1 Put 8 paper baking cases in a muffin pan, or place 8 double-layer paper cases on a cookie sheet.

2 Put the margarine, sugar, egg, flour, and cocoa in a large bowl and, using an electric hand whisk, beat together until just smooth.

3 Spoon half of the batter into the paper cases. Using a teaspoon, make an indentation in the center of each cake. Break the chocolate evenly into 8 squares and place a piece in each indentation, then spoon the remaining cake batter on top.

4 Bake the cupcakes in a preheated oven, 375°F/190°C, for 20 minutes, or until well risen and springy to the touch. Leave the cupcakes for 2–3 minutes before serving warm, dusted with sifted confectioners' sugar.

spiced chocolate muffins

ingredients

MAKES 12

3^1/$_2$ oz/100 g butter, softened

5 oz/150 g/scant ^{3}/$_4$ cup
superfine sugar

4 oz/115 g/^{1}/$_2$ cup packed
brown sugar

2 large eggs

5 fl oz/150 ml/^{2}/$_3$ cup
sour cream

5 tbsp milk

9 oz/250 g/generous
1^3/$_4$ cups all-purpose flour

1 tsp baking soda

2 tbsp unsweetened cocoa

1 tsp allspice

7 oz/200 g/generous 1 cup
semisweet chocolate chips

method

1 Line a 12-cup muffin pan with muffin liners.

2 Place the butter, superfine sugar, and brown sugar in a bowl and beat well. Beat in the eggs, sour cream, and milk until thoroughly mixed. Sift the flour, baking soda, cocoa, and allspice into a separate bowl and stir into the mixture. Add the chocolate chips and mix well. Divide the batter evenly among the paper liners. Bake in a preheated oven, 375°F/190°C, for 25–30 minutes.

3 Remove the muffins from the oven and let cool for 10 minutes. Place them on a cooling rack and let cool completely. Store in an airtight container until required.

devil's food cakes with chocolate frosting

ingredients

MAKES 18

3^1/2 tbsp soft margarine

4 oz/115 g/generous ^{1}/2 cup
   firmly packed brown sugar

2 large eggs

4 oz/115 g/generous ^{3}/4 cup
   all-purpose flour

^{1}/2 tsp baking soda

1 oz/25 g/generous ^{1}/4 cup
   unsweetened cocoa

4 fl oz/125 ml/^{1}/2 cup
   sour cream

frosting

4^1/2 oz/125 g semisweet
   chocolate

2 tbsp superfine sugar

5 fl oz/150 ml/^{2}/3 cup
   sour cream

chocolate curls
   (optional)

3^1/2 oz/100 g semisweet
   chocolate

method

1 Put 18 paper baking cases in a muffin pan, or put 18 double-layer paper cases on a cookie sheet.

2 Put the margarine, sugar, eggs, flour, baking soda, and cocoa in a large bowl and, using an electric hand whisk, beat together until just smooth. Using a metal spoon, fold in the sour cream. Spoon the batter into the paper cases.

3 Bake the cupcakes in a preheated oven, 350°F/180°C, for 20 minutes, or until well risen and firm to the touch. Transfer to a wire rack to cool.

4 To make the frosting, break the chocolate into a heatproof bowl. Set the bowl over a pan of gently simmering water and heat until melted, stirring occasionally. Remove from the heat and let cool slightly, then whisk in the sugar and sour cream until combined. Spread the frosting over the tops of the cupcakes and let set in the refrigerator before serving. If liked, serve decorated with chocolate curls made by shaving semisweet chocolate with a potato peeler.

fruit & nut squares

ingredients

MAKES 9

4 oz/115 g unsalted butter,
    plus extra for greasing

2 tbsp honey

1 egg, beaten

3 oz/85 g/generous ³/₄ cup
    ground almonds

4 oz/115 g/scant 1 cup
    no-soak dried apricots,
    finely chopped

2 oz/55 g/¹/₃ cup
    dried cherries

2 oz/55 g/generous ¹/₄ cup
    toasted chopped
    hazelnuts

1 oz/25 g/¹/₈ cup
    sesame seeds

3 oz/85 g/scant 1 cup
    rolled oats

method

1 Lightly grease a 7-inch/18-cm shallow, square baking pan with butter. Beat the remaining butter with the honey in a bowl until creamy, then beat in the egg with the almonds.

2 Add the remaining ingredients and mix together. Press into the prepared pan, ensuring that the mixture is firmly packed. Smooth the top.

3 Bake in a preheated oven, 350°F/180°C, for 20–25 minutes, or until firm to the touch and golden brown.

4 Remove from the oven and let stand for 10 minutes before marking into squares. Let stand until cold before removing from the pan. Store in an airtight container.

pecan brownies

ingredients

MAKES 20

8 oz/225 g unsalted butter,
    plus extra for greasing
2$^{1}/_{2}$ oz/70 g bittersweet
    chocolate
4$^{1}/_{2}$ oz/125 g/scant 1 cup
    all-purpose flour
$^{3}/_{4}$ tsp baking soda
$^{1}/_{4}$ tsp baking powder
2 oz/55 g/$^{1}/_{3}$ cup pecans
3$^{1}/_{2}$ oz/100 g/$^{1}/_{2}$ cup raw
    brown sugar
$^{1}/_{2}$ tsp almond extract
1 egg
1 tsp milk

method

1 Grease a large baking dish and line it with parchment paper.

2 Put the chocolate in a heatproof bowl set over a pan of gently simmering water and heat until it is melted. Meanwhile, sift together the flour, baking soda, and baking powder into a large bowl.

3 Finely chop the pecans and set aside. In a separate bowl, cream together the butter and sugar, then mix in the almond extract and the egg. Remove the chocolate from the heat and stir into the butter mixture. Add the flour mixture, milk, and chopped nuts to the bowl and stir until well combined.

4 Spoon the mixture into the prepared baking dish and smooth it. Transfer to a preheated oven, 350°F/180°C, and cook for 30 minutes, or until firm to the touch (it should still be a little soft in the center). Remove from the oven and let cool completely. Cut into 20 squares and serve.

white chocolate brownies

ingredients

MAKES 9

4 oz/115 g unsalted butter,
   plus extra for greasing

8 oz/225 g white chocolate

4 oz/115 g/³/4 cup walnut
   pieces

2 eggs

4 oz/115 g/generous ¹/2 cup
   soft brown sugar

4 oz/115 g/generous ²/3 cup
   self-rising flour

method

1 Lightly grease a 7-inch/18-cm square cake pan with butter.

2 Coarsely chop 6 oz/175 g of chocolate and all the walnuts. Put the remaining chocolate and the butter in a heatproof bowl set over a pan of gently simmering water. When melted, stir together, then set aside to cool slightly.

3 Whisk the eggs and sugar together, then beat in the cooled chocolate mixture until well mixed. Fold in the flour, chopped chocolate, and the walnuts. Turn the mixture into the prepared pan and smooth the surface.

4 Transfer the pan to a preheated oven, 350°F/180°C, and bake for 30 minutes, or until just set. The mixture should still be a little soft in the center. Remove from the oven and let cool in the pan, then cut into 9 squares before serving.

chocolate temptations

ingredients

MAKES 24

12 1/2 oz/365 g semisweet
    chocolate
6 tbsp unsalted butter, plus
    extra for greasing
1 tsp strong coffee
2 eggs
5 oz/150 g/scant 3/4 cup soft
    brown sugar
8 oz/225 g/generous 1 1/3
    cups all-purpose flour
1/4 tsp baking powder
pinch of salt
2 tsp almond extract
1 3/4 oz/50 g/scant 1/3 cup
    Brazil nuts, chopped
1 3/4 oz/50 g/scant 1/3 cup
    hazelnuts, chopped
1 1/2 oz/40 g white chocolate

method

1 Put 8 oz/225 g of the semisweet chocolate with the butter and coffee into a heatproof bowl over a pan of simmering water and heat until the chocolate is almost melted.

2 Meanwhile, beat the eggs in a bowl until fluffy. Whisk in the sugar gradually until thick. Remove the chocolate from the heat and stir until smooth. Stir it into the egg mixture until combined.

3 Sift the flour, baking powder, and salt into a bowl and stir into the chocolate mixture. Chop 3 oz/85 g of semisweet chocolate into pieces and stir into the dough. Stir in the almond extract and nuts.

4 Put 24 rounded dessertspoonfuls of the dough on a greased cookie sheet and bake in a preheated oven, 350°F/180°C, for 16 minutes. Transfer the cookies to a wire rack to cool. To decorate, melt the remaining chocolate (semisweet and white) in turn, then spoon into a piping bag and pipe lines onto the cookies.

chocolate chip oat cookies

ingredients

MAKES 20

4 oz/115 g butter, softened,
    plus extra for greasing

4 oz/115 g/$^1/_2$ cup firmly
    packed light brown sugar

1 egg

3$^1/_2$ oz/100 g/1 cup
    rolled oats

1 tbsp milk

1 tsp vanilla extract

4$^1/_2$ oz/125 g/scant 1 cup
    all-purpose flour

1 tbsp unsweetened cocoa

$^1/_2$ tsp baking powder

6 oz/175 g semisweet
    chocolate, broken
    into pieces

6 oz/175 g milk chocolate,
    broken into pieces

method

1 Place the butter and sugar in a bowl and beat together until light and fluffy. Beat in the egg, then add the oats, milk, and vanilla extract. Beat together until well blended. Sift the flour, unsweetened cocoa, and baking powder into the cookie batter and stir. Stir in the chocolate pieces.

2 Place dessertspoonfuls of the cookie batter on 2 greased cookie sheets and flatten slightly with a fork. Bake in a preheated oven, 350°F/180°C, for 15 minutes, or until slightly risen and firm. Let cool on the cookie sheets for 2 minutes, then transfer to wire racks to cool completely.

lavender cookies

ingredients

MAKES 12

2 oz/55 g/¼ cup golden
     superfine sugar, plus
     extra for dusting
1 tsp chopped lavender leaves
4 oz/115 g butter, softened,
     plus extra for greasing
finely grated rind of 1 lemon
6 oz/175 g/1¼ cups
     all-purpose flour

method

1 Place the sugar and lavender leaves in a food processor. Process until the lavender is very finely chopped, then add the butter and lemon rind and process until light and fluffy. Transfer to a large bowl. Sift in the flour and beat until the mixture forms a stiff dough.

2 Place the dough on a sheet of parchment paper and place another sheet on top. Gently press down with a rolling pin and roll out to ⅛–¼-inch/3–5-mm thick. Remove the top sheet of paper and stamp out circles from the dough using a 2¾-inch/7-cm round cookie cutter. Re-knead and re-roll the dough trimmings and stamp out more cookies.

3 Using a spatula, carefully transfer the cookies to a large, greased cookie sheet. Prick the cookies with a fork and bake in a preheated oven, 300°F/150°C, for 12 minutes, or until pale golden brown. Let cool on the cookie sheet for 2 minutes, then transfer to a wire rack to cool completely, and dust with superfine sugar.

fig & walnut cookies

ingredients

MAKES 20

3¹/₂ oz/100 g/scant ¹/₂ cup
  dried figs

8 oz/225 g unsalted butter or
  margarine, plus extra
  for greasing

4 fl oz/125 ml/¹/₃ cup
  clear honey

4 tbsp raw brown sugar

2 eggs, beaten

pinch of salt

1 tsp allspice

1 tsp baking soda

¹/₂ tsp vanilla extract

2 tbsp dried dates, finely
  chopped

8 oz/225 g/1¹/₂ cups all-
  purpose flour

8 oz/225 g/2 cups oatmeal

1 oz/25 g/generous ¹/₄ cup
  walnuts, finely chopped

dried fig pieces, to decorate
  (optional)

method

1 Finely chop the figs. Mix the butter, honey, figs, and sugar together in a large bowl. Beat the eggs into the mixture and mix thoroughly.

2 In a separate bowl, combine the salt, allspice, baking soda, vanilla extract, and dates. Gradually stir them into the creamed mixture. Sift the flour into the mixture and stir well. Finally, mix in the oatmeal and walnuts.

3 Drop 20 rounded tablespoonfuls of the mixture onto 2 large greased cookie sheets, spaced well apart to allow for spreading. Decorate with fig pieces, if using. Bake in a preheated oven, 350°F/180°C, for 10–15 minutes, or until the cookies are golden brown. Remove from the oven. Transfer to a cooling rack and let cool before serving.

oat & hazelnut morsels

ingredients

MAKES 30

6 oz/175 g unsalted butter or
   margarine, plus extra
   for greasing
8 oz/225 g/scant 1^1/$_4$ cups
   raw brown sugar
1 egg, beaten
4 tbsp milk
1 tsp vanilla extract
^{1}/$_2$ tsp almond extract
4 oz/115 g/generous ^{2}/$_3$ cup
   hazelnuts
4 oz/115 g/1 cup all-purpose
   flour
1^1/$_2$ tsp ground allspice
^{1}/$_4$ tsp baking soda
pinch of salt
8 oz/225 g/2 cups oatmeal
5 oz/140 g/scant 1 cup
   golden raisins

method

1 Cream the butter and sugar together in a mixing bowl. Blend in the egg, milk, and vanilla and almond extracts until thoroughly combined. Chop the hazelnuts finely.

2 In a mixing bowl, sift the flour, allspice, baking soda, and salt together. Add to the creamed mixture slowly, stirring constantly. Mix in the oatmeal, golden raisins, and hazelnuts.

3 Put 30 rounded tablespoonfuls of the mixture onto 2 large greased cookie sheets, spaced well apart to allow for spreading. Transfer to a preheated oven, 375°F/190°C, and bake for 12–15 minutes, or until the cookies are golden brown. Remove from the oven and place on a cooling rack to cool before serving.

desserts

Desserts were originally "invented" to make full use of produce that was only available for a very short season, long before sophisticated preserving equipment, such as the refrigerator and freezer, was invented! As a result, fruits, nuts, eggs, and dairy produce have been transformed into the most wonderful creations, becoming ever more elegant as their role changed from necessity to sheer pleasure.

Traditional fruit pies have evolved from a simple fruit filling encased in pie dough, like the Forest Fruit Pie, to some glorious variations on the theme. Toffee Apple Tart, Pear & Pecan Strudel, Pear Tart Tatin, and Blackberry Tart with Cassis Cream are delicious examples of how to make the most of nature's bounty. An alternative way to use fruit is in Peach Cobbler, with a soft batter topping, or a classic dish from France, Cherry Clafoutis—the cherries float in a creamy batter scented with vanilla extract.

Nuts are also a superb ingredient for desserts. Try Florentine Praline Tartlets, Almond Tart, Sicilian Marzipan Tart with Candied Fruit, or an old favorite, Pecan Pie. And if you can't do without chocolate, there are recipes for Chocolate Nut Strudel, Mississippi Mud Pie, Chocolate Fudge Tart, Double Chocolate Roulade, and that most unusual of baked desserts—Baked Chocolate Alaska. Heaven!

toffee apple tart

ingredients

SERVES 6

butter, for greasing

10 oz/300 g ready-made
    unsweetened pie dough

all-purpose flour, for dusting

filling

3 lb/1.3 kg Pippin or other
    firm, sweet apples,
    peeled and cored

1 tsp lemon juice

3 heaped tbsp butter

$3^1/2$ oz/100 g/$^1/2$ cup
    superfine sugar

7 oz/200 g/1 cup
    granulated sugar

$2^1/2$ fl oz/75 ml/$^1/3$ cup
    cold water

5 fl oz/150 ml/$^2/3$ cup
    heavy cream

method

1 Lightly grease a 9-inch/22-cm loose-bottom fluted tart pan. Roll out the pie dough on a lightly floured counter and line the pan with it, then roll the rolling pin over the pan to trim the excess dough. Fit a piece of parchment paper into the tart shell and fill with dried beans. Let chill in the refrigerator for 30 minutes, then bake for 10 minutes in a preheated oven, 375°F/190°C. Remove the beans and paper and return to the oven for 5 minutes.

2 Meanwhile, take 4 apples, cut each one into 8 pieces, and toss in the lemon juice. Melt the butter in a skillet and sauté the apple pieces until just starting to caramelize and brown on the edges. Remove from the skillet and let cool.

3 Slice the remaining apples thinly, put them in a pan with the superfine sugar, and cook for about 20 minutes, until soft. Spoon into the tart shell and arrange the reserved apple pieces on top in a circle. Bake for 30 minutes.

4 Put the granulated sugar and water in a pan and heat until the sugar dissolves. Boil to form a caramel. Remove from the heat and add the cream, stirring constantly to combine into toffee. Remove the tart from the oven, pour the toffee over the apples, and let chill for 1 hour. Serve with heavy cream.

chocolate nut strudel

ingredients

SERVES 6

5¹/₂ oz/150 g unsalted butter,
   plus extra for greasing
8 oz/225 g/generous 1¹/₄
   cups mixed chopped nuts
4 oz/115 g semisweet
   chocolate, chopped
4 oz/115 g milk
   chocolate, chopped
4 oz/115 g white chocolate,
   chopped
7 oz/200 g filo pastry, thawed
   if frozen
3 tbsp corn syrup
2 oz/55 g/¹/₂ cup
   confectioners' sugar
ice cream, to serve

method

1 Lightly grease a cookie sheet with butter. Set aside 1 tablespoon of the nuts. Mix the 3 types of chocolate together.

2 Place 1 sheet of filo on a clean dish towel. Melt the butter and brush the sheet of filo with the butter, drizzle with a little syrup, and sprinkle with some nuts and chocolate. Place another sheet of filo on top and repeat until you have used all the nuts and chocolate.

3 Use the dish towel to help you carefully roll up the strudel and place on the cookie sheet, drizzle with a little more syrup, and sprinkle with the reserved nuts. Bake in a preheated oven, 375°F/190°C, for 20–25 minutes. If the nuts start to brown too much, cover the strudel with a sheet of foil.

4 Sprinkle the strudel with confectioners' sugar, slice, and eat warm with ice cream.

pear & pecan strudel

ingredients

SERVES 4

2 ripe pears

4 tbsp butter

2 oz/55 g/1 cup fresh white
bread crumbs

2 oz/55 g/generous $^{1}/_{3}$ cup
shelled pecans, chopped

1 oz/25 g/scant $^{1}/_{4}$ cup
muscovado sugar

finely grated rind of
1 orange

3$^{1}/_{2}$ oz/100 g filo pastry,
thawed if frozen

6 tbsp orange
blossom honey

2 tbsp orange juice

sifted confectioners' sugar,
for dusting

strained plain yogurt, to serve
(optional)

method

1 Peel, core, and chop the pears. Melt 1 tablespoon of the butter in a skillet and gently sauté the bread crumbs until golden. Transfer the bread crumbs to a bowl and add the pears, nuts, muscovado sugar, and orange rind. Place the remaining butter in a small pan and heat until melted.

2 Set aside 1 sheet of filo pastry, keeping it well wrapped, and brush the remaining filo sheets with a little melted butter. Spoon a little of the nut filling onto 1 buttered filo sheet, leaving a 1-inch/2.5-cm margin around the edge. Build up the strudel by placing the remaining buttered filo sheets on top of the first, spreading each one with nut filling as you build up the layers. Drizzle the honey and orange juice over the top.

3 Fold the short ends over the filling, then roll up, starting at a long side. Carefully lift onto a baking sheet, with the join uppermost. Brush with any remaining melted butter and crumple the reserved sheet of filo pastry around the strudel. Bake in a preheated oven, 400°F/200°C, for 25 minutes, or until golden and crisp. Dust with sifted confectioners' sugar and serve warm with strained plain yogurt, if using.

pear tarte tatin

ingredients

SERVES 6

6 tbsp butter

4 oz/115 g/generous $^1/_2$ cup
    superfine sugar

6 pears, peeled, halved,
    and cored

all-purpose flour, for dusting

8 oz/225 g ready-made puff
    pastry

heavy cream, to serve
    (optional)

method

1 Melt the butter and sugar in an ovenproof skillet over medium heat. Stir carefully for 5 minutes until it turns to a light caramel color. Take care because it gets very hot.

2 Remove the pan from the heat, place on a heatproof surface, and arrange the pears, cut side up, in the caramel. Place one half in the center and surround it with the others.

3 On a lightly floured counter, roll out the dough to a round, slightly larger than the skillet, and place it on top of the pears. Tuck the edges down into the skillet.

4 Bake near the top of a preheated oven, 400°F/200°C, for 20–25 minutes until the pastry is well risen and golden brown. Remove from the oven and let cool for 2 minutes.

5 Invert the tart onto a serving dish that is larger than the skillet and has enough depth to take any juices that may run out. Remember that this is very hot, so use a pair of thick potholders. Serve warm, with heavy cream if using.

banana toffee pie

ingredients

SERVES 4

filling

3 x 14 oz/400 g cans
    sweetened
    condensed milk
4 ripe bananas
juice of $1/2$ lemon
1 tsp vanilla extract
16 fl oz/475 ml/
    heavy cream, whipped
$2^3/4$ oz/75 g semisweet
    chocolate, grated

cookie crust

3 oz/85 g butter, melted,
    plus extra for greasing
$5^1/2$ oz/150 g graham crackers,
    crushed into crumbs
1 oz/25 g/scant $1/3$ cup
    shelled almonds,
    toasted and ground
1 oz/25 g/scant $1/3$ cup
    shelled hazelnuts,
    toasted and ground

method

1 Place the unopened cans of milk in a large pan and add enough water to cover them. Bring to a boil, then reduce the heat and let simmer for 2 hours, topping up the water level to keep the cans covered. Carefully lift out the hot cans from the pan and let cool.

2 Place the butter in a bowl and add the crushed graham crackers and ground nuts. Mix together well, then press the mixture evenly into the base and side of a greased 9-inch/23-cm tart pan. Bake in a preheated oven, 350°F/180°C, for 10–12 minutes, then remove from the oven and let cool.

3 Peel and slice the bananas and place in a bowl. Squeeze over the juice from the lemon, add the vanilla extract, and mix together. Spread the banana mixture over the cookie crust in the pan, then spoon over the contents of the cooled cans of condensed milk.

4 Sprinkle over $1^3/4$ oz/50 g of the chocolate, then top with a layer of whipped cream. Sprinkle over the remaining grated chocolate and serve the pie at room temperature.

blackberry tart with cassis cream

ingredients

SERVES 6

pie dough

12 oz/350 g/2¼ cups
   all-purpose flour, plus
   extra for dusting
pinch of salt
6 oz/175 g unsalted butter
1¾ oz/50 g/¼ cup
   superfine sugar
cold water

filling

1 lb 10 oz/750 g blackberries
6 tbsp golden superfine sugar
1 tbsp cassis
5 tsp semolina
1 egg white

to serve

10 fl oz/300 ml/generous
   1 cup heavy cream
1 tbsp cassis
fresh mint leaves

method

1 To make the pie dough, sift the flour and salt into a large bowl and rub in the butter. Stir in the sugar and add enough cold water to bring the dough together, then wrap in plastic wrap and let chill for 30 minutes.

2 Meanwhile, rinse and pick over the blackberries, then put in a bowl with 4 tbsp of the sugar and the cassis, stirring to coat.

3 On a lightly floured counter, roll out the dough to a large circle, handling carefully because it is quite a soft dough. Leave the edges ragged and place on a cookie sheet. Sprinkle the dough with the semolina, leaving a good 2½-inch/6-cm edge. Pile the fruit into the center and brush the edges of the dough with the egg white. Fold in the edges of the dough to overlap and enclose the fruit, making sure to press together the dough in order to close any gaps. Brush with the remaining egg white, sprinkle with the remaining sugar, and bake in a preheated oven, 400°F/200°C, for 25 minutes.

4 To serve, whip the cream until it starts to thicken and stir in the cassis. Serve the tart hot, straight from the oven, with a good spoonful of the cassis cream and decorated with mint leaves.

peach cobbler

ingredients

SERVES 4–6

filling

6 peaches, peeled and sliced

4 tbsp superfine sugar

$1/2$ tbsp lemon juice

$1^1/2$ tsp cornstarch

$1/2$ tsp almond or vanilla extract

vanilla or pecan ice cream,
    to serve

pie topping

6 oz/175 g/scant $1^1/4$ cups
    all-purpose flour

4 oz/115 g/generous $1/2$ cup
    superfine sugar

$1^1/2$ tsp baking powder

$1/2$ tsp salt

3 oz/85 g butter, diced

1 egg

5–6 tbsp milk

method

1 Place the peaches in a 9-inch/23-cm square ovenproof dish that is also suitable for serving. Add the sugar, lemon juice, cornstarch, and almond extract and toss together. Bake the peaches in a preheated oven, 425°F/220°C, for 20 minutes.

2 Meanwhile, to make the topping, sift the flour, all but 2 tablespoons of the sugar, the baking powder, and salt into a bowl. Rub in the butter with the fingertips until the mixture resembles bread crumbs. Mix the egg and 5 tablespoons of the milk in a pitcher, then mix into the dry ingredients with a fork until a soft, sticky dough forms. If the dough seems too dry, stir in the extra tablespoon of milk.

3 Reduce the oven temperature to 400°F/ 200°C. Remove the peaches from the oven and drop spoonfuls of the topping over the surface, without smoothing. Sprinkle with the remaining sugar, return to the oven, and bake for an additional 15 minutes, or until the topping is golden brown and firm—the topping will spread as it cooks. Serve hot or at room temperature with ice cream.

cherry clafoutis

ingredients

SERVES 6

butter, for greasing

1 lb/450 g ripe fresh cherries, pitted

3^1/$_2$ oz/100 g/^{1}/$_2$ cup superfine sugar

2 large eggs

1 egg yolk

3^1/$_2$ oz/100 g/^{2}/$_3$ cup all-purpose flour

pinch of salt

6 fl oz/175 ml/1^3/$_4$ cups milk

4 tbsp heavy cream

1 tsp vanilla extract

method

1 Lightly grease a 40-fl oz/1.25-liter/5-cup ovenproof serving dish or a 10-inch/25-cm quiche dish. Scatter the cherries over the bottom of the prepared dish, then place the dish on a cookie sheet.

2 Using an electric mixer, whisk the sugar, eggs, and the egg yolk together until blended and a pale yellow color, scraping down the sides of the bowl as necessary.

3 Beat in the flour and salt, then slowly beat in the milk, cream, and vanilla extract until a light, smooth batter forms. Pour the batter into the dish.

4 Transfer the filled dish on the cookie sheet to a preheated oven, 400°F/200°C, and bake for 45 minutes, or until the top is golden brown and the batter is set.

5 Let the pudding stand for at least 5 minutes, then serve hot, or at room temperature.

new york cheesecake

ingredients

SERVES 8–10

6 tbsp butter

7 oz/200 g graham crackers, crushed

sunflower oil, for brushing

14 oz/400 g/1³/₄ cups cream cheese

2 large eggs

5 oz/140 g/³/₄ cup superfine sugar

1¹/₂ tsp vanilla extract

16 fl oz/450 ml/2 cups sour cream

blueberry topping

2 oz/55 g/generous ¹/₄ cup superfine sugar

4 tbsp water

9 oz/250 g/generous 1¹/₂ cups fresh blueberries

1 tsp arrowroot

method

1 Melt the butter in a pan over low heat. Stir in the crackers, then spread in an 8-inch/20-cm springform pan brushed with oil. Place the cream cheese, eggs, ¹/₂ cup of the sugar, and ¹/₂ teaspoon of the vanilla extract in a food processor. Process until smooth. Pour over the cracker base and smooth the top. Place on a cookie sheet and bake in a preheated oven, 375°F/190°C, for 20 minutes until set. Remove from the oven and leave for 20 minutes. Leave the oven switched on.

2 Mix the cream with the remaining sugar and vanilla extract in a bowl. Spoon over the cheesecake. Return it to the oven for 10 minutes, let cool, then chill in the refrigerator for 8 hours, or overnight.

3 To make the topping, place the sugar in a pan with 2 tablespoons of the water over low heat and stir until the sugar has dissolved. Increase the heat, add the blueberries, cover, and cook for a few minutes, or until they begin to soften. Remove from the heat. Mix the arrowroot and remaining water in a bowl, add to the fruit, and stir until smooth. Return to low heat. Cook until the juice thickens and turns translucent. Let cool.

4 Remove the cheesecake from the pan 1 hour before serving. Spoon the fruit topping over and let chill until ready to serve.

forest fruit pie

ingredients

SERVES 4

filling

8 oz/225 g/1⅝ cups
    blueberries
8 oz/225 g/1⅝ cups
    raspberries
8 oz/225 g/1⅝ cups
    blackberries
3½ oz/100 g/½ cup
    superfine sugar
2 tbsp confectioners' sugar,
    to decorate
whipped cream, to serve

pie dough

8 oz/225 g/1¼ cups all-
    purpose flour, plus extra
    for dusting
1 oz/25 g/generous ¼ cup
    ground hazelnuts
3½ oz/100 g butter, cut into
    small pieces, plus extra
    for greasing
finely grated rind of 1 lemon
1 egg yolk, beaten
4 tbsp milk

method

1 Place the fruit in a pan with 3 tablespoons of the superfine sugar and let simmer gently, stirring frequently, for 5 minutes. Remove the pan from the heat.

2 Sift the flour into a bowl, then add the hazelnuts. Rub in the butter with the fingertips until the mixture resembles bread crumbs, then sift in the remaining sugar. Add the lemon rind, egg yolk, and 3 tablespoons of the milk and mix. Turn out on to a lightly floured counter and knead briefly. Wrap and let chill in the refrigerator for 30 minutes.

3 Grease an 8-inch/20-cm pie dish with butter. Roll out two-thirds the pie dough to a thickness of ¼ inch/5 mm and use it to line the base and side of the dish. Spoon the fruit into the pastry shell. Brush the rim with water, then roll out the remaining pie dough to cover the pie. Trim and crimp round the edge, then make 2 small slits in the top and decorate with 2 leaf shapes cut out from the dough trimmings. Brush all over with the remaining milk. Bake in a preheated oven, 375°F/190°C, for 40 minutes.

4 Remove the pie from the oven, sprinkle with the confectioners' sugar and serve with whipped cream.

mississippi mud pie

ingredients

SERVES 8

pie dough

8 oz/225 g/1¹/₄ cups
    all-purpose flour, plus
    extra for dusting
2 tbsp unsweetened cocoa
5¹/₂ oz/150 g butter
2 tbsp superfine sugar
1–2 tbsp cold water

filling

6 oz/175 g butter
12 oz/350 g/scant 1³/₄ cups
    packed brown sugar
4 eggs, lightly beaten
4 tbsp unsweetened cocoa,
    sifted
5¹/₂ oz/150 g semisweet
    chocolate
10 fl oz/300 ml/1¹/₄ cups
    light cream
1 tsp chocolate extract

to decorate

15 fl oz/425 ml/scant 2 cups
    heavy cream, whipped
chocolate flakes and curls

method

1 To make the pie dough, sift the flour and cocoa into a mixing bowl. Rub in the butter with the fingertips until the mixture resembles fine bread crumbs. Stir in the sugar and enough cold water to mix to a soft dough. Wrap the dough and let chill in the refrigerator for 15 minutes.

2 Roll out the dough on a lightly floured counter and use to line a 9-inch/23-cm loose-bottom tart pan or ceramic pie dish. Line with parchment paper and fill with dried beans. Bake in a preheated oven, 375°F/190°C, for 15 minutes. Remove from the oven and take out the paper and beans. Bake the tart shell for an additional 10 minutes.

3 To make the filling, beat the butter and sugar together in a bowl and gradually beat in the eggs with the cocoa. Melt the chocolate and beat it into the mixture with the light cream and the chocolate extract.

4 Reduce the oven temperature to 325°F/160°C. Pour the mixture into the tart shell and bake for 45 minutes, or until the filling has set gently.

5 Let the mud pie cool completely, then transfer it to a serving plate, if you like. Cover with the whipped cream. Decorate the pie with chocolate flakes and curls and then let chill until ready to serve.

florentine praline tartlets

ingredients

MAKES 6 TARTLETS

praline

$3^1/_2$ oz/100 g/$^1/_2$ cup sugar

3 tbsp water

$1^3/_4$ oz/50 g/scant $^1/_2$ cup
    slivered almonds

butter, for greasing

pie dough

$4^1/_2$ oz/125 g/generous
    $^3/_4$ cup all-purpose flour,
    plus extra for dusting

pinch of salt

$2^1/_2$ oz/75 g cold butter,
    cut into pieces

1 tsp confectioners' sugar

cold water

frangipane

$2^1/_2$ oz/75 g butter

2 eggs

$2^3/_4$ oz/75 g/generous $^1/_3$ cup
    superfine sugar

2 tbsp all-purpose flour

4 oz/115 g/1 cup ground
    almonds

topping

8 natural candied cherries,
    chopped

2 tbsp candied peel, chopped

$3^1/_2$ oz/100 g semisweet
    chocolate, chopped

method

1 To make the praline, put the sugar and water in a pan and dissolve the sugar over low heat. Do not stir the sugar, just let it boil for 10 minutes, until it turns to caramel, then stir in the nuts and turn out onto greased foil. Let cool and harden. When cold break up the praline and chop into smallish pieces.

2 Grease 6 x $3^1/_2$-inch/9-cm loose-bottom fluted tartlet pans. Sift the flour and salt into a food processor, add the butter, and process until the mixture resembles fine bread crumbs. Add the sugar and a little cold water, and pulse to bring the dough together. Turn out onto a floured counter and divide into 6 pieces. Roll out each piece and use to line the tartlet pans. Roll the rolling pin over the pans to trim the excess dough. Put in the freezer for 30 minutes.

3 Meanwhile, make the frangipane. Melt the butter and beat the eggs and sugar together. Stir the melted butter into the egg and sugar mixture, then add the flour and almonds.

4 Bake the tartlet shells blind, straight from the freezer, for 10 minutes in a preheated oven, 400°F/200°C. Divide the frangipane among the tartlet shells and return to the oven for 8–10 minutes. Meanwhile, mix the cherries, peel, chocolate, and praline together. Divide among the tartlets while they are still hot so that some of the chocolate melts. Let cool completely.

chocolate fudge tart

ingredients

SERVES 6

12 oz/350 g ready-made
  unsweetened pie dough
flour, for sprinkling
confectioners' sugar, for
  dusting
5 fl oz/150 ml/²/₃ cup
  whipped cream and
  ground cinnamon, to
  decorate

filling

5 oz/140 g semisweet
  chocolate, finely chopped
6 oz/175 g butter, diced
12 oz/350 g/1³/₄ cups golden
  granulated sugar
3¹/₂ oz/100 g/³/₄ cup
  all-purpose flour
¹/₂ tsp vanilla extract
6 eggs, beaten

method

1 Roll out the pie dough on a lightly floured counter and use to line an 8-inch/20-cm deep loose-bottom tart pan. Prick the dough base lightly with a fork, then line with foil and fill with pie weights. Bake in a preheated oven, 400°F/200°C, for 12–15 minutes, or until the dough no longer looks raw. Remove the beans and foil and bake for an additional 10 minutes, or until the dough is firm. Let cool. Reduce the oven temperature to 350°F/180°C.

2 To make the filling, place the chocolate and butter in a heatproof bowl and set over a pan of gently simmering water until melted. Stir until smooth, then remove from the heat and let cool. Place the sugar, flour, vanilla extract, and eggs in a separate bowl and whisk until well blended. Stir in the chocolate and butter mixture.

3 Pour the filling into the tart shell and bake in the oven for 50 minutes, or until the filling is just set. Transfer to a wire rack to cool completely. Dust with confectioners' sugar before serving with whipped cream sprinkled lightly with cinnamon.

almond tart

ingredients

pie dough

10 oz/280 g/2 cups
    all-purpose flour, plus
    extra for dusting
$5^1/_2$ oz/150 g generous
    $^3/_4$ cup superfine sugar
1 tsp finely grated lemon rind
pinch of salt
$5^1/_2$ oz/150 g unsalted butter,
    chilled and cut into
    small dice, plus extra for
    greasing
1 medium egg, beaten lightly
1 tbsp chilled water

filling

6 oz/175 g unsalted butter,
    at room temperature
6 oz/175 g/generous $^3/_4$ cup
    superfine sugar
3 large eggs
6 oz/175 g/generous
    $1^1/_2$ cups finely
    ground almonds
2 tsp all-purpose flour
1 tbsp finely grated orange rind
$^1/_2$ tsp almond extract
confectioners' sugar,
    for dusting
sour cream (optional), to serve

method

1 To make the pie dough, put the flour, sugar, lemon rind, and salt in a bowl. Rub or cut in the butter until the mixture resembles fine bread crumbs. Combine the egg and water, then slowly pour into the flour, stirring with a fork until a coarse mass forms. Shape into a ball and let chill for at least 1 hour.

2 Roll out the pie dough on a lightly floured counter until $^1/_8$ inch/3 mm thick. Use to line a greased 10-inch/25-cm tart pan. Return to the refrigerator for at least 15 minutes, then cover the tart shell with foil and fill with pie weights or dried beans. Place in a preheated oven, 425°F/220°C, and bake for 12 minutes. Remove the pie weights and foil and return the tart shell to the oven for 4 minutes to dry the base. Remove from the oven and reduce the oven temperature to 400°F/200°C.

3 Meanwhile, make the filling. Beat the butter and sugar until creamy. Beat in the eggs, 1 at a time. Add the almonds, flour, orange rind, and almond extract, and beat until blended.

4 Spoon the filling into the tart shell and smooth the surface. Bake for 30–35 minutes, or until the top is golden and the tip of a knife inserted in the center comes out clean. Let cool completely on a wire rack, then dust with sifted confectioners' sugar. Serve with a spoonful of sour cream, if desired.

sicilian marzipan tart with candied fruit

ingredients

SERVES 6

pie dough

4^{1}/$_{2}$ oz/125 g/generous
^{3}/$_{4}$ cup all-purpose flour
pinch of salt
2^{1}/$_{2}$ oz/75 g cold butter,
cut into pieces
cold water

filling

10^{1}/$_{2}$ oz/300 g marzipan
6 oz/175 g/generous 1^{1}/$_{2}$
cups ground almonds
5^{1}/$_{2}$ oz/150 g unsalted butter
3^{1}/$_{2}$ oz/100 g/^{1}/$_{2}$ cup
superfine sugar
2 oz/55 g/scant ^{1}/$_{2}$ cup all-
purpose flour
2 eggs
2 oz/55 g/^{1}/$_{2}$ cup
golden raisins
2 oz/55 g/scant ^{1}/$_{3}$ cup mixed
candied peel, chopped
2 oz/55 g/scant ^{1}/$_{2}$ cup
natural candied
cherries, halved
2 oz/55 g/^{1}/$_{2}$ cup slivered
almonds

method

1 Lightly grease a 9-inch/22-cm loose-bottom fluted tart pan. Sift the flour and salt into a food processor, add the butter, and process until the mixture resembles fine bread crumbs. Add just enough cold water to bring the dough together. Turn out onto a counter dusted with more flour and roll out the dough 3¼ inches/ 8 cm larger than the pan. Lift the dough into the pan and press to fit. Roll the rolling pin over the pan to trim the excess dough. Fit a piece of parchment paper into the tart shell and fill with dried beans.

2 Let chill for 30 minutes, then bake for 10 minutes in a preheated oven, 375°F/190°C. Remove the beans and paper and bake for an additional 5 minutes. Lower the temperature to 350°F/ 180°C. Grate the marzipan straight onto the base of the warm dough.

3 Put the ground almonds, butter, and sugar in a food processor and pulse until smooth. Add 1 tbsp flour and 1 of the eggs and blend, then add another 1 tbsp flour and the other egg and blend. Finally add the remaining flour. Scoop the mixture into a bowl and stir in the golden raisins, peel, and cherries. Spoon the mixture over the marzipan, sprinkle with the slivered almonds, and bake for 40 minutes. Let cool completely to serve.

caramelized lemon tart

ingredients

SERVES 6

pie dough

3^1/$_2$ oz/100 g cold butter,
   cut into pieces, plus extra
   for greasing

7 oz/200 g/1^1/$_8$ cups
   all-purpose flour, plus
   extra for dusting

pinch of salt

2 tbsp superfine sugar

1 egg yolk

cold water

filling

5 lemons

2 eggs

10 oz/275 g/1^1/$_2$ cups
   superfine sugar

6 oz/175 g/generous
   1^1/$_2$ cups ground almonds

4 fl oz/125 ml/generous
   ^{1}/$_3$ cup heavy cream

3^1/$_2$ fl oz/100 ml/generous
   ^{1}/$_3$ cup water

method

1 Lightly grease a 9-inch/22-cm loose-bottom fluted tart pan. Sift the flour and salt into a food processor, add the butter, and process until the mixture resembles fine bread crumbs. Add the sugar and egg yolk, and just enough cold water to bring the dough together. Roll out the dough on a lightly floured counter to a circle 3^1/4 inches/8 cm larger than the pan. Lift the dough carefully into the pan, press to fit, and trim the excess dough. Fit parchment paper into the tart shell and fill with dried beans. Let chill for 30 minutes, then bake blind for 10 minutes in a preheated oven, 375°F/190°C. Remove the beans and paper and bake for 5 minutes more.

2 Put the juice and finely grated rind of 3 of the lemons in a bowl. Add the eggs, 3 oz/85 g/ ^{1}/2 cup of the sugar, the ground almonds, and the cream, whisking to combine. Pour into the tart shell and bake for 25 minutes.

3 Thinly slice the remaining 2 lemons, discarding the seeds and ends. Heat the remaining sugar and water in a pan until the sugar is dissolved. Let simmer for 5 minutes, then add the lemon slices and boil for 10 minutes. Arrange the lemon slices over the surface of the cooked tart in a spiral pattern. Drizzle over the remaining lemon syrup. Serve warm or cold.

truffled honey tart

ingredients

SERVES 6

pie dough

$2^{1}/_{2}$ oz/75 g cold butter,
cut into pieces, plus extra
for greasing
$4^{1}/_{2}$ oz/125 g/generous
$3/_4$ cup all-purpose flour,
plus extra for dusting
pinch of salt
1 tsp confectioners' sugar
cold water

filling

8 oz/225 g/1 cup curd cheese
4 oz/115 g/$^{1}/_{2}$ cup cream
cheese
4 fl oz/125 ml/$^{1}/_{2}$ cup heavy
cream
2 egg yolks, plus 1 whole egg
2 tbsp superfine sugar
4 tbsp flower honey, plus
extra for drizzling
crystallized violets or sugared
rose petals, to decorate

method

1 Lightly grease a 9-inch/22-cm loose-bottom fluted tart pan. Sift the flour and salt into a food processor, add the butter, and process until the mixture resembles fine bread crumbs. Add the sugar, and a little cold water, just enough to bring the dough together. Turn out onto a counter dusted with more flour and roll out the dough 3¼ inches/8 cm larger than the pan. Carefully lift the dough into the pan and press to fit. Roll the rolling pin over the pan to trim the excess dough. Fit a piece of parchment paper into the tart shell, fill with dried beans, and let chill in the refrigerator for 30 minutes.

2 Remove the tart shell from the refrigerator and bake blind for 10 minutes in a preheated oven, 375°F/190°C, then remove the beans and paper and bake for an additional 5 minutes.

3 Mix the curd cheese, cream cheese, and cream together until smooth, then stir in the egg yolks and whole egg, plus the sugar and honey, until completely smooth. Pour into the tart shell and bake for 30 minutes. Remove from the oven and let cool in the pan for 10 minutes. Drizzle with more honey and decorate with violets or petals.

baked chocolate alaska

ingredients

SERVES 4

butter, for greasing

2 eggs

6 oz/175 g/generous ³/₄ cup
    superfine sugar,
    plus 4 tbsp

4 tbsp all-purpose flour

2 tbsp unsweetened cocoa

3 egg whites

2 pints/1 liter/4 cups good-
    quality chocolate ice
    cream

method

1 Grease a 7-inch/18-cm round cake pan and line the base with parchment paper.

2 Whisk the eggs and the 4 tablespoons of sugar in a mixing bowl until very thick and pale. Sift the flour and cocoa together and carefully fold in.

3 Pour into the prepared pan and bake in a preheated oven, 425°F/220°C, for 7 minutes, or until springy to the touch. Turn out and transfer to a wire rack to cool completely.

4 Whisk the egg whites in a clean, greasefree bowl until soft peaks form. Gradually add the remaining sugar, whisking until you have a thick, glossy meringue. Place the sponge on a baking sheet. Soften the ice cream in the refrigerator and pile it onto the center to form a dome.

5 Pipe or spread the meringue over the ice cream, making sure it is completely enclosed. (At this point the dessert can be frozen, if wished.) Return to the oven for 5 minutes, until the meringue is a light golden brown. Serve at once.

mixed fruit pavlova

ingredients

SERVES 4

6 egg whites

pinch of cream of tartar

pinch of salt

10 oz/300 g/1^1/2 cups
superfine sugar

20 fl oz/600 ml/scant
2^1/2 cups heavy cream

1 tsp vanilla extract

2 kiwifruits, peeled and sliced

9 oz/250 g strawberries,
hulled and sliced

3 ripe peaches, sliced

1 ripe mango, peeled and
sliced

2 tbsp orange liqueur,
such as cointreau

fresh mint leaves,
to decorate

method

1 Line 3 cookie sheets with baking parchment, then draw an 8^1/2-inch/22-cm circle in the center of each one. Beat the egg whites into stiff peaks. Mix in the cream of tartar and salt. Gradually add 7 oz/200 g/1 cup of sugar. Beat for 2 minutes until glossy. Fill a pastry bag with the mixture and use it to fill each circle, making them slightly domed in the center. Bake in a preheated oven, 225°F/110°C, for 3 hours. Remove from the oven and let cool.

2 Whip together the cream and vanilla extract with the remaining sugar. Put the fruit into a separate bowl and stir in the liqueur.

3 Put one meringue circle onto a serving plate and spread over one third of the sugared cream, followed by one third of the fruit, then top with a meringue. Spread over another third of cream and another third of fruit. Top with the last meringue and spread over the remaining cream, followed by the remaining fruit. Decorate with mint leaves and serve.

pecan pie

ingredients

SERVES 8

pie dough

9 oz/250 g/scant $1^5/8$ cups
    all-purpose flour

pinch of salt

4 oz/115 g butter, cut into
    small pieces

1 tbsp lard or vegetable
    shortening, cut into
    small pieces

2 oz/55 g/generous $^1/4$ cup
    golden superfine sugar

6 tbsp cold milk

filling

3 eggs

8 oz/250 g/generous 1 cup
    muscovado sugar

1 tsp vanilla extract

pinch of salt

3 oz/85 g butter, melted

3 tbsp corn syrup

3 tbsp molasses

12 oz/350 g/2 cups shelled
    pecans, roughly chopped

pecan halves, to decorate

whipped cream or vanilla ice
    cream, to serve

method

1 To make the pie dough, sift the flour and salt into a mixing bowl and rub in the butter and lard with the fingertips until the mixture resembles fine bread crumbs. Work in the superfine sugar and add the milk. Work the mixture into a soft dough. Wrap the dough and let chill in the refrigerator for 30 minutes.

2 Roll out the pie dough and use it to line a 9–10 inch/23–25-cm tart pan. Trim off the excess by running the rolling pin over the top of the tart pan. Line with parchment paper, and fill with dried beans. Bake in a preheated oven, 400°F/200°C, for 20 minutes. Take out of the oven and remove the paper and dried beans. Reduce the oven temperature to 350°F/180°C. Place a baking sheet in the oven.

3 To make the filling, place the eggs in a bowl and beat lightly. Beat in the muscovado sugar, vanilla extract, and salt. Stir in the butter, syrup, molasses, and chopped nuts. Pour into the pastry shell and decorate with the pecan halves.

4 Place on the heated baking sheet and bake in the oven for 35-40 minutes until the filling is set. Serve warm or at room temperature with whipped cream or vanilla ice cream.

lemon meringue pie

ingredients

SERVES 8–10

butter, for greasing

all-purpose flour, for dusting

9 oz/250 g ready-made pie
    dough, thawed if frozen

3 tbsp cornstarch

3 oz/85 g/scant $^1/_2$ cup
    superfine sugar

grated rind of 3 lemons

10 fl oz/300 ml/1$^1/_4$ cups
    cold water

5 fl oz/150 ml/$^2/_3$ cup
    lemon juice

3 egg yolks

2 oz/55 g unsalted butter,
    cut into small cubes

meringue

3 egg whites

6 oz/175 g/$^3/_4$ cup superfine
    sugar

1 tsp golden granulated sugar

method

1 Grease a 10-inch/25-cm fluted tart pan. On a lightly floured counter, roll out the pie dough and ease it into the pan. Roll off the excess to neaten the tart shell. Prick the bottom of the tart shell and let chill, uncovered, for 20–30 minutes. Line the shell with parchment paper and fill with dried beans. Bake on a preheated cookie sheet in a preheated oven, 400°F/200°C, for 15 minutes. Remove the beans and paper and return to the oven for 10 minutes. Remove and reduce the temperature to 300°F/150°C.

2 Put the cornstarch, sugar, and lemon rind into a pan. Blend in a little of the water to make a smooth paste. Gradually add the remaining water and the lemon juice. Bring to a boil over medium heat, stirring continuously. Let simmer gently for 1 minute until smooth and glossy. Remove from the heat. Beat in the egg yolks, 1 at a time, then the butter. Place the pan in a bowl of cold water to cool the filling, then spoon it into the tart shell.

3 To make the meringue, whisk the egg whites until soft peaks form. Gradually add the superfine sugar, whisking well with each addition. Spoon the meringue over the filling to cover it completely. Swirl the meringue into peaks and sprinkle with granulated sugar. Bake for 20–30 minutes until the meringue is crispy and pale gold (the center should still be soft). Let cool slightly before serving.

cappuccino soufflés

ingredients

SERVES 4

6 tbsp whipping cream

2 tsp instant espresso
coffee granules

2 tbsp Kahlua

butter, for greasing

3 large eggs, separated,
plus 1 extra egg white

2 tbsp golden superfine sugar,
plus extra for coating

5^1/$_2$ oz/150 g semisweet
chocolate, melted
and cooled

unsweetened cocoa,
for dusting

vanilla ice cream and
chocolate biscuits, to
serve

method

1 Place the cream in a small, heavy-bottom pan and heat gently. Stir in the coffee until it has dissolved, then stir in the Kahlua. Divide the coffee mixture between 6 lightly greased 6 fl oz/175-ml/^{3}/$_4$-cup ramekins coated with superfine sugar.

2 Place the egg whites in a clean, greasefree bowl and whisk until soft peaks form, then gradually whisk in the sugar until stiff but not dry. Stir the egg yolks and melted chocolate together in a separate bowl, then stir in a little of the whisked egg whites. Gradually fold in the remaining egg whites.

3 Divide the mixture between the ramekins. Place the ramekins on a baking sheet and bake in a preheated oven, 375°F/190°C, for 15 minutes, or until just set. Dust with unsweetened cocoa and serve immediately with vanilla ice cream and chocolate bisuits.

double chocolate roulade

ingredients

SERVES 8

4 eggs, separated

4 oz/115 g/generous ½ cup
golden superfine sugar

4 oz/115 g semisweet
chocolate, melted
and cooled

1 tsp instant coffee granules,
dissolved in 2 tbsp hot
water, cooled

confectioners' sugar,
to decorate

unsweetened cocoa,
for dusting

fresh raspberries, to serve

filling

9 fl oz/250 ml/generous 1 cup
heavy cream

5 oz/140 g white chocolate,
broken into pieces

3 tbsp Tia Maria

method

1 Line a 9 x 13-inch/23 x 33-cm jelly roll pan with nonstick parchment paper. Whisk the egg yolks and sugar in a bowl until pale and mousse-like. Fold in the chocolate, then the coffee. Place the egg whites in a clean bowl and whisk until stiff but not dry. Stir a little of the egg whites into the chocolate mixture, then fold in the remainder. Pour into the pan and bake in a preheated oven, 350°F/180°C, for 15–20 minutes, or until firm. Cover with a damp dish towel and let stand in the pan for 8 hours, or overnight.

2 Meanwhile, make the filling. Heat the cream until almost boiling. Place the chocolate in a food processor and chop coarsely. With the motor running, pour the cream through the feed tube. Process until smooth. Stir in the Tia Maria. Transfer to a bowl and let cool. Let chill for 8 hours, or overnight.

3 To assemble the roulade, whip the chocolate cream until soft peaks form. Cut a sheet of waxed paper larger than the roulade, place on a counter and sift confectioners' sugar over it. Turn the roulade out onto the paper. Peel away the lining paper. Spread the chocolate cream over the roulade and roll up from the short side nearest to you. Transfer to a dish, seam-side down. Let chill for 2 hours, then dust with cocoa. Serve with raspberries.

baking
with yeast

Baking with yeast seems to hold terrors for those who have never tried it, and yet it is really easy, especially now that active dry yeast has largely superseded the use of fresh yeast. Yeast cooking needs a little planning because of the time required for the dough to rise, but there is absolutely nothing to beat the aroma of fresh bread wafting through your home, so the wait is more than worth it.

Sweet breads are delicious for breakfast or brunch, or with coffee or tea at any time of day. Life will never be the same once you've mastered those flaky, buttery French specialties, Croissants and Pains au Chocolate, or the slightly less messy-to-eat brioche—we've included a recipe for delicious, individual Orange & Raisin Brioches for you to try. Cinnamon Swirls and Crown Loaf are fun to eat, too—you can bite into them tidily, or unroll them to pull out the fruity bits of filling!

Savory breads are the perfect accompaniment to soups, salads, and main meals. Both sweet and savory breads are great for making sandwiches— try Apricot & Walnut Bread with a filling of cream cheese, or Olive & Sun-dried Tomato Bread packed with your favorite cold cuts and some watercress. And if you love pizza, there's a recipe for a basic Cheese & Tomato Pizza—you can dress it up all you like.

fresh croissants

ingredients

MAKES 12 CROISSANTS

1 lb 2 oz/500 g/scant 4 cups
    white bread flour, plus
    extra for dusting
1¹/₂ oz/40 g/scant ¹/₄ cup
    superfine sugar
1 tsp salt
2 tsp active dry yeast
10 fl oz/300 ml/1¹/₄ cups
    milk, heated until just
    warm to the touch
10¹/₂ oz/300 g/1¹/₄ cups
    butter, softened, flattened
    with a rolling pin between
    2 sheets of waxed paper
    to form a rectangle
    ¹/₄ inch/5 mm thick, then
    chilled in the refrigerator,
    plus extra for greasing
1 egg, lightly beaten with
    1 tbsp milk, to glaze
jelly, to serve (optional)

you will need

a cardboard triangular
    template, base 7 inches/
    18 cm and sides
    8 inches/20 cm

method

1 Stir the dry ingredients in a large bowl, make a well in the center, and add the milk. Mix to a soft dough, adding more milk if too dry. Knead on a lightly floured counter for 5–10 minutes, or until smooth and elastic. Let rise in a large, greased bowl, covered, in a warm place until doubled in size.

2 Knead the dough for 1 minute. Let the butter soften slightly. Roll out the dough on a well-floured counter to 18 x 6 inches/46 x 15 cms. Place the butter in the center. Then with the short end of the dough toward you, fold the top third down toward the center, then fold the bottom third up and squeeze the edges together gently. Rotate so that the fold is to your left and the top flap toward your right. Roll out to a rectangle and fold again. If the butter feels soft, wrap the dough in plastic wrap, and let chill. Repeat the rolling process twice more. Cut the dough in half. Roll out one half into a triangle ¹/₄ inch/5 mm thick (keep the other half refrigerated). Use the cardboard template to cut out the croissants.

3 Brush the triangles lightly with the glaze. Roll into croissant shapes, starting at the base and tucking the point underneath. Brush again with the glaze. Place on an ungreased cookie sheet and let double in size, then bake in a preheated oven, 400°F/200°C, for 15–20 minutes until golden. Serve with jelly, if liked.

orange & raisin brioches

ingredients

MAKES 12

2 oz/55 g butter, melted, plus
    extra for greasing

8 oz/225 g/generous 1$^{1}/_{2}$ cups
    strong white bread flour,
    plus extra for dusting

$^{1}/_{2}$ tsp salt

2 tsp active dry yeast

1 tbsp golden superfine sugar

2 oz/55 g/$^{1}/_{3}$ cup raisins

grated rind of 1 orange

2 tbsp tepid water

2 eggs, beaten

vegetable oil, for oiling

1 beaten egg, for glazing

method

1 Grease 12 individual brioche molds. Sift the flour and salt into a warmed bowl and stir in the yeast, sugar, raisins, and orange rind. Make a well in the center. In a separate bowl, mix together the water, eggs, and melted butter and pour into the dry ingredients. Beat vigorously to make a soft dough. Turn out onto a lightly floured counter and knead for 5 minutes, or until smooth and elastic. Brush a clean bowl with oil. Place the dough in the bowl, cover with plastic wrap, and let stand in a warm place for 1 hour, or until doubled in size.

2 Turn out onto a floured counter, knead lightly for 1 minute, then roll into a rope shape. Cut into 12 equal pieces. Shape three-fourths of each piece into a ball and place in the prepared molds. With a floured finger, press a hole in the center of each. Shape the remaining pieces of dough into little plugs and press into the holes, flattening the top slightly.

3 Place the molds on a cookie sheet, cover lightly with oiled plastic wrap, and let stand in a warm place for 1 hour, until the dough comes almost to the top.

4 Brush the brioches with beaten egg and bake in a preheated oven, 425°F/220°C, for 15 minutes, or until golden brown. Serve warm with butter, if you like.

pains au chocolat

ingredients

MAKES 8

3¹/₂ oz/100 g butter, plus
    extra for greasing
9 oz/250 g/scant 2 cups
    white bread flour, plus
    extra for dusting
1 tsp salt
2 tsp active dry yeast
6 fl oz/175 ml/³/₄ cup milk
2 tbsp golden superfine sugar
1 tbsp oil, plus extra for
    brushing
4 oz/115 g semisweet
    chocolate, coarsely
    chopped
1 egg yolk and 2 tbsp milk,
    for glazing

method

1 Grease a cookie sheet. Sift the flour and salt into a bowl and stir in the yeast. Make a well in the center. Heat the milk in a pan until tepid. Add the sugar and oil and stir until the sugar has dissolved. Stir into the flour and mix well. Turn the dough out onto a lightly floured counter and knead until smooth, then place in an oiled bowl. Cover and let rise in a warm place for 2–3 hours, or until doubled in size.

2 Knead on a floured counter and roll into a rectangle 3 times as long as it is wide. Divide the butter into thirds. Dot one portion over the top two-thirds of the dough, leaving a ¹/₂-inch/ 1-cm margin round the edges. Fold the lower third up and the top third down. Seal the edges. Give the dough a half-turn. Roll into a rectangle. Repeat the process twice, then fold in half. Put into an oiled plastic bag. Let chill for 1 hour.

3 Cut the dough in half and roll out into 2 rectangles of 12 x 6 inches/30 x 15 cm. Cut each half into 4 rectangles of 6 x 3 inches/ 15 x 7.5 cm. Sprinkle chocolate along one short end of each and roll up. Place on the cookie sheet in a warm place for 2–3 hours, or until doubled in size. To glaze, mix the egg yolk and milk and brush over the rolls. Bake in a preheated oven, 425°F/220°C, for 15–20 minutes, or until golden and well risen.

chocolate bread

ingredients

MAKES 1 LOAF

butter, for greasing

1 lb/450 g/3$\frac{1}{2}$ cups strong
    white bread flour, plus
    extra for dusting

1 oz/25 g/generous $\frac{1}{4}$ cup
    unsweetened cocoa

1 tsp salt

$\frac{1}{4}$-oz/7-g envelope active
    dry yeast

2 tbsp brown sugar

1 tbsp corn oil

10 fl oz/300 ml/1$\frac{1}{4}$ cups
    lukewarm water

butter, to serve

method

1 Lightly grease a 2-lb/900-g loaf pan with a little butter. Sift the flour and cocoa into a large bowl. Stir in the salt, yeast, and brown sugar. Pour in the oil and water and mix together to form a dough.

2 Knead the dough on a lightly floured counter for 5 minutes. Alternatively, use an electric mixer with a dough hook. Place the dough in a greased bowl, cover, and let rise in a warm place for 1 hour, or until doubled in size.

3 Punch down the dough and shape it into a loaf. Place the dough in the pan, cover, and let stand in a warm place for an additional 30 minutes.

4 Bake the bread in a preheated oven, 400°F/200°C, for 25–30 minutes, or until a hollow sound is heard when the bottom of the bread is tapped. Transfer the bread to a wire rack and let cool completely. Cut into slices and serve with butter.

citrus bread

ingredients

MAKES 1 LOAF

4 tbsp butter, diced, plus
    extra for greasing
1 lb/450 g/3^1/$_2$ cups strong
    white bread flour, plus
    extra for dusting
^{1}/$_2$ tsp salt
1^3/$_4$ oz/50 g/^{1}/$_4$ cup superfine
    sugar
1 envelope active dry yeast
5–6 tbsp orange juice, plus
    grated rind of 1 orange
4 tbsp lemon juice, plus
    grated rind of 1 lemon
3–4 tbsp lime juice, plus
    grated rind of 1 lime
5 fl oz/150 ml/^{2}/$_3$ cup
    lukewarm water
2 tbsp honey, for glazing

method

1 Lightly grease a cookie sheet with butter.

2 Sift the flour and salt into a large mixing bowl. Stir in the sugar and dry yeast. Rub in the butter with your fingertips until the mixture resembles bread crumbs. Add all of the fruit juices and the water and bring together with your fingers to form a dough.

3 Place the dough on a lightly floured counter and knead for 5 minutes. Alternatively, use an electric mixer with a dough hook. Place the dough in a greased bowl, cover, and let rise in a warm place for 1 hour, until doubled in size.

4 Meanwhile, grate the rind of the orange, lemon, and lime. Knead the fruit rinds into the dough.

5 Divide the dough into 2 balls, making one slightly bigger than the other. Place the larger ball on the cookie sheet and set the smaller one on top. Push a floured finger through the center of the dough. Cover and let rise for about 40 minutes,or until springy to the touch.

6 Bake in a preheated oven, 425°F/220°C, for 35 minutes. Remove from the oven and transfer to a wire rack. Glaze with the honey and let cool completely.

stollen

ingredients

SERVES 10

3 oz/85 g/generous ¹/₂ cup
currants

2 oz/55 g/¹/₃ cup raisins

2 tbsp chopped candied peel

2 oz/55 g/¹/₃ cup candied
cherries, rinsed,
dried, and quartered

2 tbsp rum

2 oz/55 g butter

6 fl oz/175 ml/³/₄ cup milk

2 tbsp golden superfine sugar

13 oz/375 g/generous 2³/₄
cups strong white bread
flour, plus extra for dusting

¹/₂ tsp ground nutmeg

¹/₂ tsp ground cinnamon

seeds from 3 cardamoms

2 tsp active dry yeast

finely grated rind of 1 lemon

1 egg, beaten

1¹/₂ oz/40 g/scant ¹/₂ cup
slivered almonds

vegetable oil, for brushing

6 oz/175 g marzipan

melted butter, for brushing

sifted confectioners' sugar,
for dredging

method

1 Place the currants, raisins, peel, and cherries in a bowl, stir in the rum and set aside. Place the butter, milk, and sugar in a pan over low heat and stir until the sugar dissolves and the butter melts. Cool until lukewarm. Sift the flour, nutmeg, and cinnamon into a bowl. Crush the cardamom seeds and add them. Stir in the yeast. Make a well in the center, stir in the milk mixture, lemon rind, and egg and beat into a dough.

2 Turn the dough out onto a floured counter. Knead for 5 minutes, adding more flour if necessary. Knead in the soaked fruit and the almonds. Transfer to a clean, oiled bowl. Cover with plastic wrap and let stand in a warm place for up to 3 hours, or until doubled in size. Turn out onto a floured counter, knead for 1–2 minutes, then roll out to a 10-inch/25-cm square.

3 Roll the marzipan into a sausage shorter than the length of the dough. Place in the center. Fold the dough over the marzipan, overlapping it. Seal the ends. Place seam-side down on a greased cookie sheet, cover with oiled plastic wrap, and let stand in a warm place for up to 2 hours, or until doubled in size. Preheat the oven to 375°F/190°C. Bake for 40 minutes, or until golden and hollow sounding when tapped. Brush with melted butter, dredge with confectioners' sugar, and let cool on a wire rack.

cinnamon swirls

ingredients

SERVES 12

2 tbsp butter, cut into small
    pieces, plus
    extra for greasing
8 oz/225 g/1$^1/_2$ cups strong
    white bread flour
$^1/_2$ tsp salt
$^1/_4$-oz/7-g envelope active
    dry yeast
1 egg, beaten
4 fl oz/125 ml/$^1/_2$ cup
    warm milk
2 tbsp maple syrup

filling

4 tbsp butter, softened
2 tsp ground cinnamon
1$^3/_4$ oz/50 g/$^1/_4$ cup firmly
    packed brown sugar
1$^3/_4$ oz/50 g/generous $^1/_4$ cup
    currants

method

1 Grease a 9-inch/23-cm square cake pan. Sift the flour and salt into a bowl. Stir in the yeast. Rub in the butter with your fingertips until the mixture resembles fine bread crumbs. Add the egg and milk and mix to form a dough. Place in a greased bowl, cover, and let stand in a warm place for 40 minutes, or until doubled in size.

2 Knead the dough lightly for 1 minute to punch it down, then roll out on a lightly floured counter to form a rectangle measuring 12 x 9 inches/30 x 23 cm.

3 To make the filling, beat the butter, cinnamon, and brown sugar together until the mixture is light and fluffy. Spread the filling over the dough, leaving a 1-inch/2.5-cm border all round. Sprinkle over the currants.

4 Carefully roll up the dough like a jelly roll, starting at a long edge, and press down to seal. Using a sharp knife, cut the roll into 12 slices. Place them in the prepared pan, cover, and let stand for 30 minutes.

5 Bake the swirls in a preheated oven, 375°F/190°C, for 20–30 minutes, or until well risen. Brush the swirls with the syrup and let cool slightly before serving warm.

crown loaf

ingredients

MAKES 1 LOAF

2 tbsp butter, diced, plus extra for greasing

8 oz/225 g/generous 1¹/₂ cups strong white bread flour, plus extra for dusting

¹/₂ tsp salt

1 envelope active dry yeast

4 fl oz/125 ml/¹/₂ cup lukewarm milk

1 egg, beaten lightly

filling

4 tbsp butter, softened

1³/₄ oz/50 g/¹/₄ cup brown sugar

2 tbsp chopped hazelnuts

1 tbsp chopped preserved ginger

1³/₄ oz/50 g/¹/₃ cup candied peel

1 tbsp rum or brandy

frosting

3¹/₂ oz/100 g/1 cup confectioners' sugar

2 tbsp lemon juice

method

1 Grease a cookie sheet with a little butter. Sift the flour and salt into a large mixing bowl. Stir in the yeast. Rub in the butter with your fingertips. Add the milk and egg and bring together with your fingers to form a dough.

2 Place the dough in a greased bowl, cover, and let stand in a warm place for about 40 minutes, until doubled in size. Punch down the dough lightly for 1 minute, then roll out into a rectangle measuring 12 x 9 inches/ 30 x 23 cm.

3 To make the filling, cream the butter and sugar together in a large bowl until light and fluffy. Stir in the hazelnuts, ginger, candied peel, and rum or brandy. Spread the filling over the dough, leaving a 1-inch/2.5-cm border around the edges.

4 Roll up the dough, starting from one of the long edges, into a sausage shape. Cut into slices at 2-inch/5-cm intervals and place the slices in a circle on the cookie sheet, sides just touching. Cover and stand in a warm place to rise for 30 minutes.

5 Bake in a preheated oven, 325°F/190°C, for 20–30 minutes or until golden. Meanwhile, mix the confectioners' sugar with enough lemon juice to form a thin frosting. Let the loaf cool slightly before drizzling with frosting. Let the frosting set slightly before serving.

date & honey loaf

ingredients

SERVES 10

butter, for greasing

9 oz/250 g/1¾ cups strong
   white bread flour, plus
   extra for dusting

2¾ oz/75 g/½ cup strong
   brown bread flour

½ tsp salt

¼-oz/7-g envelope active
   dry yeast

7 fl oz/200 ml/scant 1 cup
   lukewarm water

3 tbsp corn oil

3 tbsp honey

2¾ oz/75 g/½ cup dried
   dates, chopped

2 tbsp sesame seeds

method

1 Grease a 2-lb/900-g loaf pan with butter. Sift the white and brown flours into a large bowl and stir in the salt and yeast. Pour in the water, oil, and honey and mix to form a dough.

2 Place the dough on a lightly floured counter and knead for 5 minutes, or until smooth, then place in a greased bowl. Cover and let rise in a warm place for 1 hour, or until doubled in size.

3 Knead in the dates and sesame seeds. Shape the dough and place in the prepared pan. Cover and let stand in a warm place for an additional 30 minutes, or until springy to the touch.

4 Bake the loaf in a preheated oven, 425°F/ 220°C, for 30 minutes, or until the bottom of the loaf sounds hollow when tapped. Transfer to a wire rack and let cool completely. Serve cut into thick slices.

banana & orange bread

ingredients

MAKES 1 MEDIUM LOAF

1 lb 2 oz/500 g/scant 4 cups
    white bread flour, plus
    an extra 1–2 tbsp for
    sticky dough, and for
    dusting

1 tsp salt

1 tsp active dry yeast

3 tbsp butter, diced

2 medium ripe bananas
    or 1 large ripe banana,
    peeled and mashed

3 tbsp runny honey

4 tbsp orange juice

7 fl oz/200 ml/scant 1 cup
    hand-hot buttermilk

vegetable oil, for oiling

milk, to glaze (optional)

method

1 Place the flour, salt, and yeast in a large bowl. Rub in the butter and add the mashed bananas and honey. Make a well in the center and gradually work in the the orange juice and buttermilk to make a smooth dough.

2 Turn the dough out onto a lightly floured counter and knead for 5–7 minutes, or until the dough is smooth and elastic. If the dough looks very sticky, add a little more white bread flour. (The stickiness depends on the ripeness and size of the bananas.) Place the dough in an oiled bowl, cover with plastic wrap, and leave in a warm place to rise for 1 hour, or until it has doubled in size.

3 Oil a 2-lb/900-g loaf pan. Turn the dough out onto a lightly floured counter and knead for 1 minute until smooth. Shape the dough to the length of the pan and three times the width. Fold the dough into three lengthwise and place it in the pan with the join underneath. Cover and let stand in a warm place for 30 minutes until it has risen above the pan.

4 Just before baking, brush the milk over the loaf to glaze, if desired. Bake in a preheated oven, 425°F/220°C, for 30 minutes, or until firm and golden brown. Test that the loaf is cooked by tapping it on the bottom—it should sound hollow. Transfer to a wire rack to cool completely before serving.

mango twist bread

ingredients

MAKES 1 LOAF

3 tbsp butter, diced, plus
   extra for greasing
1 lb/450 g/3$\frac{1}{2}$ cups strong
   white bread flour, plus
   extra for dusting
1 tsp salt
1 envelope active dry yeast
1 tsp ground ginger
1$\frac{3}{4}$ oz/50 g/$\frac{1}{4}$ cup brown
   sugar
1 small mango, peeled,
   pitted, and blended to
   a paste
9 fl oz/250 ml/1 cup
   lukewarm water
2 tbsp honey
4$\frac{1}{2}$ oz/125 g/$\frac{2}{3}$ cup
   golden raisins
1 egg, beaten lightly
confectioners' sugar,
   for dusting

method

1 Grease a cookie sheet with a little butter. Sift the flour and salt into a mixing bowl, stir in the dry yeast, ginger, and brown sugar and rub in the butter with your fingertips until the mixture resembles bread crumbs.

2 Stir in the mango paste, lukewarm water, and honey and bring together to form a dough.

3 Place the dough on a lightly floured counter. Knead for about 5 minutes, until smooth. Alternatively, use an electric mixer with a dough hook. Place the dough in a greased bowl, cover, and let rise in a warm place for about 1 hour, until it has doubled in size.

4 Knead in the golden raisins and shape the dough into 2 rope shapes, each 10 inches/ 25 cm long. Carefully twist the 2 pieces together and pinch the ends to seal. Place the dough on the cookie sheet, cover, and let stand in a warm place for an additional 40 minutes.

5 Brush the loaf with the egg. Bake in a preheated oven, 425°F/220°C, for 30 minutes, or until golden. Let cool on a wire rack and dust with confectioners' sugar before serving.

apricot & walnut bread

ingredients

SERVES 12

2 oz/55 g butter, plus extra
    for greasing

12 oz/350 g/generous 2^1/$_2$
    cups strong white bread
    flour, plus extra for dusting

^{1}/$_2$ tsp salt

1 tsp golden superfine sugar

2 tsp active dry yeast

4 oz/115 g/generous ^{2}/$_3$ cup
    no-soak dried apricots,
    chopped

2 oz/55 g/^{1}/$_3$ cup chopped
    walnuts

5 fl oz/150 ml/^{2}/$_3$ cup
    tepid milk

2^1/$_2$ fl oz/75 ml/scant ^{1}/$_3$ cup
    tepid water

1 egg, beaten

vegetable oil, for brushing

topping

3 oz/85 g/generous ^{3}/$_4$ cup
    confectioners' sugar

a little water

walnut halves

method

1 Grease and flour a cookie sheet. Sift the flour and salt into a warmed bowl and stir in the sugar and yeast. Rub in the butter and add the chopped apricots and walnuts. Make a well in the center. In a separate bowl, mix together the milk, water, and egg. Pour into the dry ingredients and mix to a soft dough. Turn out onto a floured counter and knead for 10 minutes, or until smooth. Place the dough in a clean bowl brushed with oil, cover with oiled plastic wrap, and let stand in a warm place for 2–3 hours, or until doubled in size.

2 Turn the dough out onto a floured counter and knead lightly for 1 minute. Divide into 5 equal pieces and roll each piece into a rope 12-inches/30-cm long. Braid 3 ropes together, pinching the ends to seal, and place on the prepared cookie sheet. Twist the remaining 2 ropes together and place on top. Cover lightly with oiled plastic wrap and let stand in a warm place for 1–2 hours, or until doubled in size.

3 Bake the bread in a preheated oven, 425°F/220°C, for 10 minutes, then reduce the heat to 375°F/190°C, and bake for an additional 20 minutes. Transfer to a wire rack to cool. To make the topping, sift the confectioners' sugar into a bowl, stir in enough water to make a thin frosting and drizzle over the loaf. Decorate with walnuts.

crusty white bread

ingredients

MAKES 1 MEDIUM LOAF

1 egg

1 egg yolk

hand-hot water, as required

1 lb 2 oz/500 g/scant 4 cups
white bread flour, plus
extra for dusting

1 1/2 tsp salt

2 tsp sugar

1 tsp active dry yeast

2 tbsp butter, diced

vegetable oil, for oiling

method

1 Place the egg and egg yolk in a pitcher and beat lightly to mix. Add enough hand-hot water to make up to 10 fl oz/300 ml/1 1/4 cups. Stir well.

2 Place the flour, salt, sugar, and yeast in a large bowl. Add the butter and rub it in with your fingertips until the mixture resembles bread crumbs. Make a well in the center, add the egg mixture, and work to a smooth dough.

3 Turn the dough out onto a lightly floured counter and knead for 10 minutes, or until the dough is smooth and elastic. Place the dough in an oiled bowl, cover with plastic wrap, and leave in a warm place to rise for 1 hour, or until it has doubled in size.

4 Oil a loaf pan. Turn the dough out onto a lightly floured counter and knead for 1 minute until smooth. Shape the dough to the length of the pan and three times the width. Fold the dough into three lengthwise and place it in the pan with the join underneath. Cover and leave in a warm place for 30 minutes until it has risen above the pan.

5 Bake in a preheated oven, 425°F/220°C, for 30 minutes, or until firm and golden brown. Test that the loaf is cooked by tapping it on the bottom—it should sound hollow. Transfer to a wire rack to cool completely.

olive & sun-dried tomato bread

ingredients

SERVES 8

14 oz/400 g/generous
    2³/4 cups all-purpose flour,
    plus extra for dusting

1 tsp salt

1 envelope active dry yeast

1 tsp brown sugar

1 tbsp chopped fresh thyme

7 fl oz/200 ml/scant 1 cup
    warm water (heated to
    122°F/50°C)

1³/4 oz/50 g/¹/3 cup black
    olives, pitted and sliced

1³/4 oz/50 g/¹/3 cup green
    olives, pitted and sliced

3¹/2 oz/100 g/scant ¹/2 cup
    sun-dried tomatoes in oil,
    drained and sliced

4 tbsp olive oil, plus
    extra for oiling

1 egg yolk, beaten

method

1 Place the flour, salt, and yeast in a bowl and mix together, then stir in the sugar and thyme. Make a well in the center. Slowly stir in enough warm water and oil to make a dough. Mix in the olives and sun-dried tomatoes. Knead the dough for 5 minutes, then form it into a ball. Brush a bowl with oil, add the dough, and cover with plastic wrap. Let rise in a warm place for about 1¹/2 hours, or until it has doubled in size.

2 Dust a cookie sheet with flour. Knead the dough lightly, then cut into two halves and shape into ovals or circles. Place them on the cookie sheet, cover with plastic wrap, and let rise again in a warm place for 45 minutes, or until they have doubled in size.

3 Make 3 shallow diagonal cuts on the top of each piece of dough. Brush with the egg. Bake in a preheated oven, 400°F/200°C, for 40 minutes, or until cooked through—they should be golden on top and sound hollow when tapped on the bottom. Transfer to wire racks to cool. Store in an airtight container for up to 3 days.

black olive focaccia

ingredients

SERVES 12

1 lb 2 oz/500 g/scant 4 cups
    strong white bread flour,
    plus extra for dusting

1 tsp salt

2 tsp active dry yeast

12 fl oz/350 ml/1¹/₂ cups
    tepid water

6 tbsp extra-virgin olive oil,
    plus extra for oiling

4 oz/115 g/²/₃ cup pitted
    black olives, coarsely
    chopped

1 tsp rock salt

method

1 Sift the flour and salt into a warmed bowl and stir in the yeast. Pour in the water and 2 tablespoons of the olive oil and mix to a soft dough. Knead the dough on a lightly floured counter for 5–10 minutes, or until it becomes smooth and elastic. Transfer it to a clean, warmed, oiled bowl and cover with plastic wrap. Let stand in a warm place for 1 hour, or until the dough has doubled in size.

2 Brush 2 cookie sheets with oil. Punch the dough to knock out the air, then knead on a lightly floured counter for 1 minute. Add the olives and knead until combined. Divide the dough in half and shape into 2 oval shapes 11 x 9 inches/28 x 23 cm long, and place on the prepared cookie sheets. Cover with oiled plastic wrap and let stand in a warm place for 1 hour, or until the dough is puffy.

3 Press your fingers into the dough to make dimples, drizzle over 2 tablespoons of oil, and sprinkle with the rock salt. Bake in a preheated oven, 400°F/200°C, for 30–35 minutes, or until golden. Drizzle with the remaining olive oil and cover with a cloth, to give a soft crust. Slice each loaf into 6 pieces and serve warm.

focaccia with roasted cherry tomatoes, basil & crispy pancetta

ingredients

SERVES 4–6

1 lb 2 oz/500 g/scant 4 cups white bread flour, plus extra for kneading and rolling, and for dusting

1 tbsp dried basil

$^1/_2$ tsp sugar

2 tsp rapid-rise dried yeast

2 tsp salt

11 fl oz/325 ml/generous 1$^1/_4$ cups water, lukewarm

2 tbsp olive oil, plus extra for oiling

topping

14 oz/400 g cherry tomatoes

1 tbsp olive oil, plus extra for oiling and drizzling

salt and pepper

7 oz/200 g thick pancetta, diced

4 tbsp chopped fresh basil

method

1 Place the flour, dried basil, sugar, yeast, and salt in a bowl. Combine the water and oil and mix with the dry ingredients to form a soft dough, adding more water if the dough appears too dry. Turn out onto a lightly floured counter and knead for 10 minutes, or until the dough is smooth and elastic. Place in a lightly oiled bowl and cover with plastic wrap. Let stand in a warm place for 1 hour, or until doubled in size.

2 Place the tomatoes on a cookie sheet covered with parchment paper, sprinkle with oil, and season with salt and pepper. Bake in a preheated oven, 275°F/140°C, for 30 minutes, or until the tomatoes are soft.

3 Increase the oven temperature to 425°F/220°C. Remove the dough from the bowl and knead again briefly. Shape into a rectangle and place on a lightly oiled cookie sheet, turning the dough over to oil both sides. Make rough indentations in the dough using your fingers. Top with the tomatoes and pancetta. Sprinkle with salt and pepper. Let stand in a warm place for 10 minutes for the dough to rise again. Bake for 15–20 minutes, or until golden brown and cooked through. Drizzle with oil and top with fresh basil. Serve warm.

mixed seed bread

ingredients

MAKES MEDIUM 1 LOAF

13 oz/375 g/generous
     2^1/$_2$ cups white bread
     flour, plus extra for dusting
4^1/$_2$ oz/125 g/scant 1^1/$_2$ cups
     rye flour
1^1/$_2$ tbsp skim milk powder
1^1/$_2$ tsp salt
1 tbsp brown sugar
1 tsp active dry yeast
1^1/$_2$ tbsp sunflower oil, plus
     extra for oiling
2 tsp lemon juice
10 fl oz/300 ml/1^1/$_4$ cups
     hand-hot water
1 tsp caraway seeds
^{1}/$_2$ tsp poppy seeds
^{1}/$_2$ tsp sesame seeds

topping

1 egg white
1 tbsp water
1 tbsp sunflower or pumpkin
     seeds

method

1 Place the flours, milk powder, salt, sugar, and yeast in a large bowl. Pour in the oil and add the lemon juice and water. Stir in the seeds and mix well to make a smooth dough.

2 Turn the dough out onto a lightly floured counter and knead for 10 minutes, or until the dough is smooth and elastic. Place the dough in an oiled bowl, cover with plastic wrap, and let stand in a warm place to rise for 1 hour, or until it has doubled in size.

3 Oil a 2-lb/900-g loaf pan. Turn the dough out onto a lightly floured counter and knead for 1 minute until smooth. Shape the dough to the length of the pan and three times the width. Fold the dough into three lengthwise and place it in the pan with the join underneath. Cover and let stand in a warm place for 30 minutes until it has risen above the pan.

4 For the topping, lightly beat the egg white with the water to make a glaze. Just before baking, brush the glaze over the loaf, then gently press the sunflower or pumpkin seeds all over the top.

5 Bake in a preheated oven, 425°F/220°C, for 30 minutes, or until firm and golden brown. Test that the loaf is cooked by tapping it on the bottom—it should sound hollow. Transfer to a wire rack to cool completely before serving.

cheese & chive braid

ingredients

SERVES 10

1 lb/450 g/3$^{1}/_{2}$ cups strong
    white bread flour, plus
    extra for dusting

1 tsp salt

1 tsp superfine sugar

1$^{1}/_{2}$ tsp active dry yeast

2 tbsp butter

4 oz/115 g/generous 1 cup
    coarsely grated Cheddar
    cheese

3 tbsp snipped fresh chives

4 scallions, chopped

5 fl oz/150 ml/$^{2}/_{3}$ cup
    tepid milk

6 fl oz/175 ml/$^{3}/_{4}$ cup
    tepid water

vegetable oil, for oiling

beaten egg, for glazing

method

1 Sift the flour and salt into a warmed bowl and stir in the sugar and yeast. Rub in the butter, then stir in the cheese, chives, and scallions. Make a well in the center. Mix together the milk and water, pour into the well, and mix to make a soft dough. Turn the dough out onto a lightly floured counter and knead for 10 minutes, or until smooth and elastic.

2 Transfer the dough to a clean, oiled bowl and cover with plastic wrap. Let stand in a warm place for 1 hour, or until doubled in size. Brush a large cookie sheet with oil. Turn the dough out onto a floured counter and knead for 1 minute. Divide the dough into 3 pieces. Roll out each piece into a rope shape and braid the 3 pieces together, pinching the ends to seal.

3 Place on the prepared cookie sheet and cover with oiled plastic wrap. Let stand in a warm place for 45 minutes, or until doubled in size. Brush with beaten egg and bake in a preheated oven, 425°F/220°C, for 20 minutes.

4 Reduce the oven temperature to 350°F/ 180°C and bake for an additional 15 minutes, or until golden brown and the loaf sounds hollow when tapped on the bottom. Serve warm or cold.

english muffins

ingredients

MAKES 10–12

2 x $^1/_4$-oz/7-g packages
    active dry yeast

9 fl oz/250 ml/1 cup
    tepid water

4 fl oz/125 ml/$^1/_2$ cup
    natural yogurt

1 lb/450 g/3$^1/_2$ cups strong
    plain flour

$^1/_2$ tsp salt

1$^3/_4$ oz/50 g/$^1/_4$ cup fine
    semolina

oil, for greasing

butter and jelly (optional), to
    serve

method

1 Mix the yeast with half the tepid water in a bowl until it has dissolved. Add the remaining water and the yogurt and mix well.

2 Sift the flour into a large bowl and add the salt. Pour in the yeast liquid and mix well to a soft dough. Turn out onto a floured counter and knead well until very smooth. Put the dough back into the bowl, cover with plastic wrap, and let rise for 30–40 minutes in a warm place until it has doubled in size.

3 Turn out again onto the counter and knead lightly. Roll out the dough to a thickness of ¾ inch/2 cm. Using a 3-inch/7.5-cm cutter, cut into rounds and scatter the semolina over each muffin. Re-roll the trimmings of the dough and make further muffins until it is all used up. Place them on a lightly floured baking sheet, cover, and let rise again for 30–40 minutes.

4 Heat a large skillet and lightly grease with a little oil. Cook half the muffins for 7–8 minutes on each side, taking care not to burn them. Repeat with the rest of the muffins. Serve at once with lots of butter and jelly, if liked.

cheese & tomato pizza

ingredients

SERVES 2

dough

8 oz/225 g/1^1/$_2$ cups all-
purpose flour, plus extra
for dusting

1 tsp salt

1 tsp active dry yeast

1 tbsp olive oil, plus extra for
oiling

6 tbsp lukewarm water

topping

6 tomatoes, sliced thinly

6 oz/175 g mozzarella
cheese, drained and
sliced thinly

salt and pepper

2 tbsp shredded fresh basil
leaves

2 tbsp olive oil

method

1 To make the pizza dough, sift the flour and salt into a bowl and stir in the yeast. Make a well in the center and pour in the oil and water. Gradually incorporate the dry ingredients into the liquid, using a wooden spoon or floured hands.

2 Turn out the dough onto a lightly floured counter and knead well for 5 minutes, until smooth and elastic. Return to the clean bowl, cover with lightly oiled plastic wrap, and set aside to rise in a warm place for about 1 hour, or until doubled in size.

3 Turn out the dough onto a lightly floured counter and knock down. Knead briefly, then cut it in half and roll out each piece into a circle about ¼ inch/5 mm thick. Transfer to a lightly oiled cookie sheet and push up the edges with your fingers to form a small rim.

4 For the topping, arrange the tomato and mozzarella slices alternately over the pizza bases. Season with salt and pepper, sprinkle with the basil, and drizzle with the olive oil. Bake in a preheated oven, 450°F/230°C, for 15–20 minutes, until the crust is crisp and the cheese has melted. Serve immediately.

blinis

ingredients

MAKES 8

4 oz/115 g/³/₄ cup
   buckwheat flour

4 oz/115 g/³/₄ cup
   white bread flour

¹/₄-oz/7-g envelope
   active dry yeast

1 tsp salt

13 fl oz/375 ml/scant
   1³/₄ cups tepid milk

2 eggs, 1 whole and
   1 separated

vegetable oil, for brushing

sour cream and smoked
   salmon, to serve

method

1 Sift both flours into a large, warmed bowl. Stir in the yeast and salt. Beat in the milk, whole egg, and egg yolk until smooth. Cover the bowl and let stand in a warm place for 1 hour.

2 Place the egg white in a spotlessly clean bowl and whisk until soft peaks form. Fold into the batter. Brush a heavy-bottom skillet with oil and set over medium–high heat. When the skillet is hot, pour enough of the batter onto the surface to make a blini about the size of a saucer.

3 When bubbles rise, turn the blini over with a spatula and cook the other side until light brown. Wrap in a clean dish towel to keep warm while cooking the remainder. Serve the warm blinis with sour cream and smoked salmon.

savory nibbles

This chapter has recipes for some really creative and exciting savory tarts and tartlets, which will please your family and wow your guests at a lunch or supper party; savory muffins, great for lunchbags or taking on picnics; and crisp little bites to serve as appetizers with drinks.

Making pie dough can be a chore if time is short, so you can use ready-made pie dough for the savory tarts if this is more convenient. However, the Spring Vegetable Tart and the Yellow Zucchini Tart have a little Parmesan cheese in the pie dough, and this really adds a special touch, so try to make this if you can. Tartlets are especially good for serving at a buffet—they are all delicious, and Artichoke & Pancetta, Smoked Salmon, Dill & Horseradish, and Feta & Spinach are particularly stylish.

You can pack a lot of goodness into a muffin, so they are great for snacks—Leek & Ham Muffins, Herb Muffins with Smoked Cheese, and Sour Cream Muffins with Chives will appeal to younger children, and the others to those with a more sophisticated taste!

Home-baked savory nibbles are so impressive—serve Spiced Cocktail Bites, Pesto Palmiers, or Cheese & Rosemary Bites to get a dinner party off to an excellent start!

triple tomato tart

ingredients

SERVES 6

all-purpose flour, for dusting

9 oz/250 g ready-made puff
    pastry

topping

3 tbsp sundried tomato paste

9 oz/250 g ripe vine
    tomatoes, sliced

$5^1/_2$ oz/150 g cherry tomatoes,
    cut in half

2 sprigs fresh rosemary

2 tbsp extra-virgin olive oil

1 tbsp balsamic vinegar

1 egg yolk

$4^1/_2$ oz/125 g Italian sliced
    salami, chopped

salt and pepper

handful thyme sprigs

method

1 On a lightly floured counter, roll out the dough to form a rectangle 14 inches/36 cm long and 10 inches/25 cm wide and lift onto a heavy-duty cookie sheet. Spread the sundried tomato paste over the dough, leaving a $1^1/4$-inch/3-cm margin round the edge. Arrange the vine tomato slices over the tomato paste, sprinkle over the cherry tomato halves and top with the rosemary. Drizzle with 1 tablespoon of the olive oil and the balsamic vinegar.

2 Brush the edges of the dough with the egg yolk and bake in a preheated oven, 375°F/190°C, for 10 minutes. Sprinkle over the chopped salami and bake for an additional 10–15 minutes.

3 Remove the tart from the oven and season with salt and pepper. Drizzle with the remaining olive oil and sprinkle with the thyme.

crab & watercress tart

ingredients

SERVES 6

pie dough

4¹/₂ oz/125 g/generous
    ³/₄ cup all-purpose flour
pinch of salt
2¹/₂ oz/75 g cold butter,
    cut into pieces
cold water

filling

10¹/₂ oz/300 g prepared white
    and brown crabmeat
1 bunch watercress, washed
    and leaves picked from
    stems
2 fl oz/50 ml/¹/₄ cup milk
2 large eggs, plus 3 egg yolks
7 fl oz/200 ml/scant 1 cup
    heavy cream
salt and pepper
¹/₂ tsp ground nutmeg
¹/₂ bunch fresh chives, snipped
2 tbsp finely grated Parmesan
    cheese
fresh sprigs of watercress, to
    garnish

method

1 Lightly grease a 9-inch/22-cm loose-bottom fluted tart pan. Sift the flour and salt into a food processor, add the butter, and process until the mixture resembles fine bread crumbs. Add just enough cold water to bring the dough together.

2 Turn out onto a floured counter and roll out the dough 3¹/4 inches/8 cm larger than the pan. Carefully lift the dough into the pan and press to fit. Roll the rolling pin over the pan to neaten the edges and trim the excess dough. Fit a piece of parchment paper into the tart shell, fill with dried beans, and let chill in the refrigerator for 30 minutes.

3 Remove the pastry shell from the refrigerator and bake blind for 10 minutes in a preheated oven, 375°F/190°C, then remove the beans and paper. Return to the oven for 5 minutes. Remove the pan from the oven and lower the oven temperature to 325°F/160°C.

4 Arrange the crabmeat and watercress in the tart pan. Whisk the milk, eggs, and egg yolks together in a bowl. Bring the cream to simmering point in a pan and pour over the egg mixture, whisking all the time. Season with salt, pepper, and nutmeg and stir in the chives. Carefully pour this mixture over the crab and watercress and sprinkle over the Parmesan. Bake for 35–40 minutes, until golden and set. Let the tart stand for 10 minutes before serving with sprigs of watercress.

goat cheese & thyme tart

ingredients

SERVES 6

9 oz/250 g ready-made puff
pastry

topping

1 lb 2 oz/500 g goat cheese,
such as chèvre, sliced

3–4 sprigs fresh thyme,
leaves picked from stalks

2 oz/55 g/scant $^1/_3$ cup
black olives, pitted

1$^3/_4$ oz/50 g tinned anchovies
in olive oil

1 tbsp olive oil

salt and pepper

1 egg yolk

fresh sprigs of thyme, to
garnish

method

1 Roll the dough into a large circle or rectangle and place on a baking sheet.

2 Arrange the cheese slices on the dough, leaving a 1-inch/2.5-cm margin round the edge. Sprinkle the thyme and olives, then arrange the anchovies, over the cheese. Drizzle over the olive oil. Season well with salt and pepper and brush the edges of the dough with the egg yolk.

3 Bake in a preheated oven, 375°F/190°C, for 20–25 minutes, until the cheese is bubbling and the pastry is browned. Garnish with fresh sprigs of thyme.

spring vegetable tart

ingredients

SERVES 6

pie dough

9 oz/250 g/1³/₄ cups
   all-purpose flour
pinch of salt
4¹/₂ oz/125 g cold butter,
   cut into pieces
2 oz/55 g/¹/₂ cup grated
   Parmesan cheese
1 egg
cold water

filling

11 oz/300 g selection of baby
   spring vegetables, such as
   carrots, asparagus, peas,
   fava beans, scallions, corn
   cobs, and leeks, trimmed
   and peeled where
   necessary
10 fl oz/300 ml/1¹/₄ cups
   heavy cream
4¹/₂ oz/125 g sharp Cheddar
   cheese, grated
2 eggs plus 3 egg yolks
salt and pepper
handful fresh tarragon and
   flatleaf parsley, chopped

method

1 Grease a 10-inch/25-cm loose-bottom tart pan. Sift the flour and salt into a food processor, add the butter, and pulse to combine, then tip into a large bowl and add the Parmesan cheese. Mix the egg and water together in a small bowl. Add most of the egg mixture and work into a soft dough, using more egg mixture if needed. Turn out onto a floured counter and roll out the dough 3¹/₄ inches/8 cm larger than the pan. Carefully lift the dough into the pan and press to fit. Roll the rolling pin over the pan to trim the excess dough. Fit a piece of parchment paper into the tart shell, fill with dried beans, and let chill in the refrigerator for 30 minutes.

2 Bake the tart shell blind for 15 minutes in a preheated oven, 400°F/200°C, then remove the beans and paper and bake for an additional 5 minutes. Remove from the oven and let cool. Lower the oven temperature to 350°F/180°C.

3 Cut the vegetables into bite-size pieces and blanch in boiling water. Drain and let cool. Bring the cream to simmering point in a pan. Place the cheese, eggs, and egg yolks in a heatproof bowl and pour the warm cream over the mixture. Stir to combine, season well, and stir in the herbs. Arrange the vegetables in the tart shell, pour over the cheese filling, and bake for 30–40 minutes, until set. Let cool in the pan for 10 minutes before serving.

yellow zucchini tart

ingredients

SERVES 6

butter, for greasing

1 quantity cheese pie dough
(see page 200)

all-purpose flour, for dusting

filling

2 large yellow zucchini

1 tbsp salt

3 heaped tbsp unsalted
butter

1 bunch scallions, trimmed
and finely sliced

5 fl oz/150 ml/^{2}/$_3$ cup
heavy cream

3 large eggs

salt and white pepper

1 small bunch fresh chives,
chopped

method

1 Grease a 10-inch/25-cm loose-bottom tart pan. On a lightly floured counter, roll out the pie dough 3^1/$_4$ inches/8 cm larger than the pan. Carefully lift the dough into the pan and press to fit. Roll the rolling pin over the pan to neaten the edges and trim the excess dough. Fit a piece of parchment paper into the tart shell, fill with dried beans, and let chill in the refrigerator for 30 minutes.

2 Bake the tart shell blind for 15 minutes in a preheated oven, 400°F/200°C, then remove the beans and paper and bake for an additional 5 minutes. Remove from the oven and let cool. Lower the oven temperature to 350°F/180°C.

3 Meanwhile, grate the zucchini and put in a strainer with 1 tablespoon of salt. Let drain for 20 minutes, then rinse and put in a clean dish towel, squeezing all the moisture from the zucchini. Keep dry.

4 Melt the butter in a wide skillet, sauté the scallions until soft, then add the zucchini and cook over medium heat for 5 minutes, until any liquid has evaporated. Let cool slightly. Whisk together the cream, eggs, salt, pepper, and chives. Spoon the zucchini into the tart shell and pour in the cream mixture, making sure it settles properly, then bake for 30 minutes. Serve hot or cold.

squash, sage & gorgonzola tart

ingredients

SERVES 6

butter, for greasing

1 quantity pie dough
(see page 196)

all-purpose flour, for dusting

filling

1/2 small butternut squash or
1 slice pumpkin, weighing
9 oz/250 g

1 tsp olive oil

9 fl oz/250 ml/generous 1 cup
heavy cream

salt and pepper

6 oz/175 g Gorgonzola cheese

2 eggs, plus 1 egg yolk

6–8 fresh sage leaves

method

1 Cut the squash in half and brush the cut side with the oil. Place cut-side up on a cookie sheet and bake for 30–40 minutes, until browned and very soft. Let cool. Remove the seeds and scoop out the flesh into a large bowl, discarding the skin.

2 Lightly grease a 9-inch/22-cm loose-bottom fluted tart pan. On a lightly floured counter, roll out the pie dough 3 1/4 inches/8 cm larger than the pan. Lift the dough into the pan and press to fit. Roll the rolling pin over the pan to trim the excess dough. Fit a piece of parchment paper into the tart shell and fill it with dried beans. Let chill in the refrigerator for 30 minutes, then bake blind for 10 minutes in a preheated oven, 375°F/190°C. Remove the beans and paper and return to the oven for 5 minutes.

3 Mash the squash and mix it with half the cream, season with salt and pepper, then spread it in the tart shell. Slice the cheese and lay it on top. Whisk the remaining cream with the eggs and egg yolk and pour the mixture into the tart pan, making sure it settles evenly. Arrange the sage leaves on the surface. Bake for 30–35 minutes and leave for 10 minutes in the pan before serving.

artichoke & pancetta tartlets

ingredients

MAKES 6 TARTLETS

butter, for greasing
1 quantity pie dough
   (see page 196)
all-purpose flour, for dusting

filling

5 tbsp heavy cream
4 tbsp bottled artichoke paste
salt and pepper
14 oz/400 g canned artichoke
   hearts, drained
12 thin-cut pancetta slices
arugula leaves
1^3/$_4$ oz/50 g Parmesan or
   romano cheese
2 tbsp olive oil, for drizzling

method

1 Grease 6 x 3^1/$_2$-inch/9-cm loose-bottom fluted tartlet pans. Divide the pie dough into 6 pieces. On a lightly floured counter, roll each piece to fit the tartlet pans. Carefully fit each piece of dough into its pan and press well to fit. Roll the rolling pin over the pan to trim the excess dough. Cut 6 pieces of parchment paper and fit a piece into each tartlet, fill with dried beans, and let chill in the refrigerator for 30 minutes.

2 Bake the tartlet shells for 10 minutes in a preheated oven, 400°F/200°C, and then remove from the oven and take out the beans and parchment paper.

3 Meanwhile, stir the cream and the artichoke paste together and season well with salt and pepper. Divide among the tartlet shells, spreading out to cover the base of each tartlet. Cut each artichoke heart into 3 pieces and divide among the tartlets. Curl 2 slices of the pancetta into each tartlet and bake for 10 minutes.

4 To serve, top each tartlet with arugula, then, using a potato peeler, sprinkle shavings of the Parmesan cheese over the tartlets, drizzle with olive oil, and serve at once.

smoked salmon, dill & horseradish tartlets

ingredients

MAKES 6 TARTLETS

1 quantity pie dough
   (see page 196)

filling

4 fl oz/125 ml/^{1}/$_2$ cup sour
   cream
1 tsp creamed horseradish
^{1}/$_2$ tsp lemon juice
1 tsp Spanish capers,
   chopped
salt and pepper
3 egg yolks
7 oz/200 g smoked salmon
   trimmings
bunch fresh dill, chopped

method

1 Grease 6 x 3^1/$_2$-inch/9-cm loose-bottom fluted tart pans. Divide the pie dough into 6 pieces. Roll each piece to fit the tart pans. Carefully fit each piece of dough in its shell and press well to fit the pan. Roll the rolling pin over the pan to trim the excess dough. Cut 6 pieces of parchment paper and fit a piece into each tart, fill with dried beans, and let chill in the refrigerator for 30 minutes.

2 Bake the tart shells for 10 minutes in a preheated oven, 400°F/200°C, and then remove the beans and parchment paper.

3 Meanwhile, put the sour cream, horseradish, lemon juice, capers, and salt and pepper into a bowl and mix well. Add the egg yolks, the smoked salmon, and the dill and carefully mix again. Divide this mixture between the tart shells and return to the oven for 10 minutes. Let cool in the pans for 5 minutes before serving.

bleu cheese & walnut tartlets

ingredients

MAKES 12 TARTLETS

pie dough

$3^1/2$ oz/100 g cold butter, cut into pieces, plus extra for greasing

9 oz/250 g/$1^1/2$ cups all-purpose flour, plus extra for dusting

pinch of celery salt

$1^1/2$ oz/40 g/$^1/4$ cup walnut halves, chopped in a food processor

cold water

filling

2 tbsp butter

2 celery stalks, trimmed and finely chopped

1 small leek, trimmed and finely chopped

7 fl oz/200 ml/scant 1 cup heavy cream, plus 2 tbsp

7 oz/200 g bleu cheese

salt and pepper

3 egg yolks

chopped fresh parsley, to garnish

method

1 Lightly grease a 3-inch/7.5-cm 12-cup muffin pan. Sift the flour and celery salt into a food processor, add the butter, and process until the mixture resembles fine bread crumbs. Tip the mixture into a bowl. Add the walnuts and enough cold water to bring the dough together.

2 Turn out onto a floured counter and cut the dough in half. Roll out the first piece and cut out 6 x $3^1/2$-inch/9-cm circles. Roll out each circle to a $4^1/2$-inch/12-cm diameter and press into the muffin cups. Repeat with the remaining dough. Put a piece of parchment paper in each cup and fill with dried beans. Let chill in the refrigerator for 30 minutes, then bake for 10 minutes in a preheated oven, 400°F/200°C. Remove the paper and beans.

3 Melt the butter in a skillet, add the celery and leek, and cook for 15 minutes, until soft. Add 2 tablespoons of heavy cream and crumble in the bleu cheese. Mix well and season with salt and pepper. Bring the remaining cream to simmering point in a pan, then pour onto the egg yolks, stirring. Add the bleu cheese mixture, mix well, and spoon into the tartlet shells. Bake for 10 minutes, then turn the pan round in the oven and bake for an additional 5 minutes. Let cool in the pan for 5 minutes and sprinkle with parsley.

feta & spinach tartlets

ingredients

MAKES 6 TARTLETS

1 quantity pie dough
   (see page 196) with
   $1/2$ nutmeg, freshly grated,
   added to the flour

filling

8 oz/225 g/6 cups baby
   spinach
2 tbsp butter
salt and pepper
5 fl oz/150 ml/$2/3$ cup
   heavy cream
3 egg yolks
$4^{1}/2$ oz/125 g feta cheese
1 oz/25 g/scant $1/3$ cup
   pine nuts
cherry tomatoes and sprigs of
   flat-leaf parsley, to garnish

method

1 Grease 6 x 3$^{1}/2$-inch/9-cm loose-bottom fluted tart pans. Divide the pie dough into 6 pieces. Roll each piece to fit the tart pans. Carefully fit each piece of dough in its shell and press well to fit the pan. Roll the rolling pin over the pan to trim the excess dough. Cut 6 pieces of parchment paper and fit a piece into each tart, fill with dried beans, and let chill in the refrigerator for 30 minutes.

2 Bake the tart shells for 10 minutes in a preheated oven, 400°F/200°C, and then remove the beans and parchment paper.

3 Blanch the spinach in boiling water for just 1 minute, then drain, and press to squeeze all the water out. Chop the spinach. Melt the butter in a skillet, add the spinach, and cook gently to evaporate any remaining liquid. Season well with salt and pepper. Stir in the cream and egg yolks. Crumble the feta and divide between the tarts, top with the creamed spinach, and bake for 10 minutes. Sprinkle the pine nuts over the tartlets and cook for an additional 5 minutes. Garnish with cherry tomatoes and sprigs of flat-leaf parsley.

cherry tomato & poppy seed tartlets

ingredients

MAKES 12 TARTLETS

pie dough

3^1/$_2$ oz/100 g cold butter,
  cut into pieces, plus extra
  for greasing
7 oz/200 g/1^1/$_2$ cups
  all-purpose flour, plus
  extra for dusting
pinch of salt
2 tsp poppy seeds
cold water

filling

24 cherry tomatoes
1 tbsp olive oil
2 tbsp unsalted butter
2 tbsp all-purpose flour
9 fl oz/250 ml/generous 1 cup
  milk
salt and pepper
1^3/$_4$ oz/50 g sharp Cheddar
  cheese
3^1/$_2$ oz/100 g/scant ^{1}/$_2$ cup
  cream cheese
12 fresh basil leaves

method

1 Lightly grease a 3-inch/7.5-cm 12-cup muffin pan. Sift the flour and salt into a food processor, add the butter, and process until the mixture resembles fine bread crumbs. Tip the mixture into a large bowl and add the poppy seeds and a just enough cold water to bring the dough together.

2 Turn out onto a floured counter and cut the dough in half. Roll out the first piece and cut out 6 x 3^1/$_2$-inch/9-cm circles. Roll out each circle to a 4^1/$_2$-inch/12-cm diameter and press into the muffin cups. Repeat with the remaining dough. Put a piece of parchment paper in each cup and fill with dried beans. Let chill in the refrigerator for 30 minutes, then bake blind for 10 minutes in a preheated oven, 400°F/200°C. Remove the paper and beans.

3 Put the tomatoes in an ovenproof dish, drizzle with the olive oil, and roast for 5 minutes.

4 Melt the butter in a pan, stir in the flour, and cook for 5–8 minutes. Gradually add the milk, stirring, and cook for an additional 5 minutes. Season well and stir in the cheeses until well combined. Put 2 tomatoes in each tartlet shell and spoon in the cheese sauce, then put back into the oven for 15 minutes. Remove from the oven and top each tartlet with a basil leaf.

eggplant, pesto & prosciutto tartlets

ingredients

MAKES 6 TARTLETS

all-purpose flour, for dusting
9 oz/250 g ready-made puff
    pastry

filling

1 large or 2 small eggplants,
    trimmed and thinly sliced
5 tbsp olive oil
3 buffalo Mozzarella cheeses,
    sliced
6 tbsp pesto
pepper
1 egg yolk
6 slices prosciutto

method

1 Roll out the puff pastry on a lightly floured counter and divide into 6 pieces. Roll each piece into circles or rectangles, then place on 2 cookie sheets, 3 on each.

2 Brush the eggplant slices with 2 tablespoons of the olive oil and cook briefly in a nonstick skillet, in batches, then arrange the slices neatly overlapping on each dough base, leaving a 1-inch/2.5-cm margin round the edges. Lay the mozzarella slices over the eggplant slices and spoon over the pesto. Drizzle with the remaining olive oil and season with pepper.

3 Brush the edges of the dough with egg yolk and bake in a preheated oven, 375°F/190°C, for 15 minutes. Remove from the oven and drape a slice of prosciutto on each tartlet before serving.

spicy chicken muffins

ingredients

MAKES 12

4 fl oz/125 ml/^{1}/$_2$ cup
   sunflower or peanut oil,
   plus extra for oiling

2 onions, chopped

3 scallions, chopped

1 small fresh red chile,
   seeded and finely
   chopped

3 skinless, boneless
   chicken thighs, chopped
   into small pieces

1 tsp paprika

10^1/$_2$ oz/300 g/scant 2^1/$_4$ cups
   self-rising flour

1 tsp baking powder

2 large eggs

1 tbsp lemon juice

1 tbsp grated lemon rind

4 fl oz/125 ml/^{1}/$_2$ cup sour
   cream

4 fl oz/125 ml/^{1}/$_2$ cup plain
   yogurt

salt and pepper

method

1 Oil a 12-cup muffin pan with sunflower oil. Heat a little of the remaining oil in a skillet, add the onions, scallions, and chile, and cook over low heat, stirring constantly, for 3 minutes. Remove from the heat, lift out the onions, scallions, and chile, and set aside. Heat a little more of the remaining oil in the skillet, add the chicken and paprika, and cook, stirring, over medium heat for 5 minutes. Remove from the heat and set aside.

2 Sift the flour and baking powder into a large mixing bowl. In a separate bowl, lightly beat the eggs, then stir in the remaining oil and the lemon juice and rind. Pour in the sour cream and the yogurt and mix together. Add the egg mixture to the flour mixture, then gently stir in the onions, scallions, chile, and chicken. Season with salt and pepper. Do not overstir the batter—it is fine for it to be a little lumpy.

3 Divide the muffin batter evenly among the 12 cups in the muffin pan (they should reach the top), then transfer to a preheated oven, 375°F/190°C. Bake for 20 minutes, or until risen and golden. Remove the muffins from the oven and serve warm, or place them on a cooling rack and let cool.

leek & ham muffins

ingredients

MAKES 12

2 tbsp sunflower or peanut
   oil, plus extra for oiling
   (if using)
1 leek, washed, trimmed,
   and finely chopped
10 oz/280 g/2 cups
   all-purpose flour
2 tsp baking powder
1/2 tsp baking soda
1 large egg, lightly beaten
10 fl oz/300 ml/1 1/4 cups
   thick strained plain yogurt
4 tbsp butter, melted
1 oz/25 g Cheddar cheese,
   grated
1 oz/25 g fresh chives,
   finely snipped
5 1/2 oz/150 g cooked ham,
   chopped

method

1 Oil a 12-cup muffin pan with sunflower oil, or line it with 12 muffin paper liners. Heat the remaining oil in a skillet, add the chopped leek, and cook, stirring, over low heat for 2 minutes. Remove from the heat and let cool.

2 Sift the flour, baking powder, and baking soda into a large mixing bowl. In a separate bowl, lightly mix the egg, yogurt, and melted butter together. Add the Cheddar cheese, chives, cooked leek, and half of the chopped ham, then mix together well. Add the cheese mixture to the flour mixture, then gently stir together until just combined. Do not overstir the batter—it is fine for it to be a little lumpy.

3 Divide the muffin batter evenly among the 12 cups in the muffin pan or the paper liners (they should be about two-thirds full). Sprinkle over the remaining chopped ham, then transfer to a preheated oven, 400°F/200°C. Bake for 20 minutes, or until risen and golden. Remove the muffins from the oven and serve warm, or place them on a cooling rack and let cool.

potato & pancetta muffins

ingredients

MAKES 12

1 tbsp sunflower or peanut
    oil, plus extra for oiling
    (if using)

3 shallots, finely chopped

12 oz/350 g/scant 2^1/$_2$ cups
    self-rising flour

1 tsp salt

1 lb/450 g potatoes, cooked
    and mashed

2 large eggs

12 fl oz/350 ml/1^1/$_2$ cups milk

4 fl oz/125 ml/^{1}/$_2$ cup sour
    cream

1 tbsp finely snipped
    fresh chives

5^1/$_2$ oz/150 g pancetta,
    broiled and crumbled
    into pieces

4 tbsp grated Cheddar
    cheese

method

1 Oil a 12-cup muffin pan with sunflower oil, or line it with 12 muffin paper liners. Heat the remaining oil in a skillet, add the chopped shallots, and cook, stirring, over low heat for 2 minutes. Remove from the heat and let cool.

2 Sift the flour and salt into a large mixing bowl. In a separate bowl, mix the potatoes, eggs, milk, sour cream, chives, and half of the pancetta together. Add the potato mixture to the flour mixture and then gently stir together until just combined. Do not overstir the batter—it is fine for it to be a little lumpy.

3 Divide the muffin batter evenly among the 12 cups in the muffin pan or the paper liners (they should be about two-thirds full). Sprinkle over the remaining pancetta, then sprinkle over the cheese. Transfer to a preheated oven, 400°F/200°C, and bake for 20 minutes, or until risen and golden. Remove the muffins from the oven and serve warm, or place them on a cooling rack and let cool.

crab & cream cheese muffins

ingredients

MAKES 12

1 tbsp sunflower or peanut
   oil, for oiling (if using)
10 oz/280 g/2 cups
   all-purpose flour
1^1/$_2$ tsp baking powder
^{1}/$_2$ tsp baking soda
^{1}/$_2$ tsp salt
1 large egg
5 fl oz/150 ml/^{2}/$_3$ cup
   plain yogurt
5 fl oz/150 ml/^{2}/$_3$ cup
   sour cream
1 oz/25 g Cheddar cheese,
   grated
1 oz/25 g/scant ^{1}/$_2$ cup
   chopped fresh parsley
1 oz/25 g/scant ^{1}/$_2$ cup
   chopped fresh dill

crab & cream cheese filling

7 oz/200 g canned crabmeat,
   drained
8 oz/225 g/scant 1 cup
   cream cheese
2 tbsp mayonnaise
salt and pepper

method

1 Oil a 12-cup muffin pan with sunflower oil, or line it with 12 muffin paper liners. Sift the flour, baking powder, baking soda, and salt into a large mixing bowl.

2 In a separate bowl, lightly beat the egg, then pour in the yogurt and sour cream and mix together. Stir in the grated cheese and chopped herbs. Add the sour cream and cheese mixture to the flour mixture, then gently stir together. Do not overstir the batter—it is fine for it to be a little lumpy.

3 Divide the muffin batter evenly among the 12 cups in the muffin pan or the paper liners (they should be about two-thirds full), then transfer to a preheated oven, 400°F/200°C. Bake for 20 minutes, or until risen and golden.

4 Meanwhile, make the filling. Place the crabmeat in a mixing bowl and flake with a fork. Add the cream cheese and mayonnaise, mix together well and season well. Cover the bowl with plastic wrap and let chill.

5 Transfer the cooked muffins to a cooling rack and let cool to room temperature. Cut them in half horizontally. Spread the crabmeat filling over the bottom halves of the muffins. Replace the top halves, so that the filling is sandwiched in the middle, and serve.

herb muffins with smoked cheese

ingredients

MAKES 12

1 tbsp sunflower or peanut
  oil, for oiling (if using)
10 oz/280 g/2 cups
  all-purpose flour
2 tsp baking powder
$1/2$ tsp baking soda
1 oz/25 g smoked hard
  cheese, grated
$1^3/4$ oz/50 g/scant $3/4$ cup
  fresh parsley, finely
  chopped
1 large egg, lightly beaten
10 fl oz/300 ml/$1^1/4$ cups
  thick strained plain yogurt
4 tbsp butter, melted

method

1 Oil a 12-cup muffin pan with sunflower oil, or line it with 12 muffin paper liners. Sift the flour, baking powder, and baking soda into a large mixing bowl. Add the smoked cheese and the parsley and mix together well.

2 In a separate bowl, lightly mix the egg, yogurt, and melted butter together. Add the yogurt mixture to the flour mixture and then gently stir together until just combined. Do not overstir the batter—it is fine for it to be a little lumpy.

3 Divide the muffin batter evenly among the 12 cups in the muffin pan or the paper liners (they should be about two-thirds full), then transfer to a preheated oven, 400°F/200°C. Bake for 20 minutes, or until risen and golden. Remove the muffins from the oven and serve warm, or place them on a cooling rack and let cool.

sour cream muffins with chives

ingredients

MAKES 12

1 tbsp sunflower or peanut oil, for oiling (if using)

10 oz/280 g/2 cups all-purpose flour

2 tsp baking powder

$^1/_2$ tsp baking soda

1 oz/25 g Cheddar cheese, grated

1$^1/_4$ oz/35 g fresh chives, finely snipped, plus extra to garnish

1 large egg, lightly beaten

7 fl oz/200 ml/scant 1 cup sour cream

3$^1/_2$ fl oz/100 ml/generous $^1/_3$ cup plain unsweetened yogurt

4 tbsp butter, melted

method

1 Oil a 12-cup muffin pan with sunflower oil, or line it with 12 muffin paper liners. Sift the flour, baking powder, and baking soda into a large mixing bowl. Add the cheese and chives and mix together well.

2 In a separate bowl, lightly mix the egg, sour cream, yogurt, and melted butter together. Add the sour cream mixture to the flour mixture and then gently stir together until just combined. Do not overstir the batter—it is fine for it to be a little lumpy.

3 Divide the muffin batter evenly among the 12 cups in the muffin pan or the paper liners (they should be about two-thirds full). Sprinkle over the remaining snipped chives to garnish and transfer to a preheated oven, 400°F/ 200°C. Bake for 20 minutes, or until risen and golden. Remove the muffins from the oven and serve warm, or place them on a cooling rack and let cool.

spiced cocktail bites

ingredients

MAKES ABOUT 20

4 oz/115 g butter, plus extra
   for greasing

5 oz/140 g/1 cup all-purpose
   flour, plus extra for dusting

2 tsp curry powder

3 oz/85 g/generous ³/₄ cup
   grated Cheddar cheese

2 tsp poppy seeds

1 tsp black onion seeds

1 egg yolk

cumin seeds, for sprinkling

method

1 Grease 2 cookie sheets with a little butter. Sift the flour and curry powder into a bowl. Cut the butter into pieces and add to the flour. Rub in until the mixture resembles bread crumbs, then stir in the cheese, poppy seeds, and black onion seeds. Stir in the egg yolk and mix to a firm dough.

2 Wrap the dough in plastic wrap and let chill in the refrigerator for 30 minutes. On a floured counter, roll out the dough to ^{1}/8-inch/3-mm thick. Stamp out shapes with a cutter. Re-roll the trimmings and stamp out more cookies until the dough is used up.

3 Place the cookies on the prepared cookie sheets and sprinkle with the cumin seeds. Let chill for an additional 15 minutes. Bake in a preheated oven, 375°F/190°C, for 20 minutes, or until crisp and golden. Serve warm or transfer to wire racks to cool.

curried cheese bites

ingredients

MAKES 40

$3^1/_2$ oz/100 g butter, softened,
    plus extra for greasing
$3^1/_2$ oz/100 g/$^3/_4$ cup
    all-purpose flour,
    plus extra for dusting
1 tsp salt
2 tsp curry powder
$3^1/_2$ oz/100 g/1 cup grated
    mellow semihard cheese
$3^1/_2$ oz/100 g/1 cup freshly
    grated Parmesan cheese

method

1 Lightly grease about 4 cookie sheets with a little butter.

2 Sift the flour and salt into a mixing bowl. Stir in the curry powder and both the grated cheeses. Rub in the softened butter with your fingertips, then bring the mixture together to form a soft dough.

3 Roll out the dough thinly on a lightly floured counter to form a rectangle. Cut out 40 circles using a 2-inch/5-cm cookie cutter and arrange on the cookie sheets. Bake in a preheated oven, 350°F/180°C, for 10–15 minutes, until golden brown.

4 Let the curried cheese bites cool slightly on the cookie sheets, then transfer them to a wire rack to cool completely and crispen.

pesto palmiers

ingredients

MAKES 20

butter, for greasing

all-purpose flour, for dusting

9 oz/250 g ready-made
   puff pastry

3 tbsp green or red pesto

1 egg yolk, beaten with
   1 tbsp water

1 oz/25 g/$1/4$ cup freshly
   grated Parmesan cheese

sprigs of fresh basil, to
   garnish

method

1 Grease a cookie sheet with a little butter. On a floured counter, roll out the pastry to a 14 x 6-inch/35 x 15-cm rectangle and trim the edges with a sharp knife. Spread the pesto evenly over the pastry. Roll up the ends tightly to meet in the center of the pastry.

2 Wrap in plastic wrap and let chill in the refrigerator for 20 minutes, until firm, then remove from the refrigerator and unwrap. Brush with the beaten egg yolk on all sides. Cut across into $1/2$-inch/1-cm thick slices. Place the slices on the prepared cookie sheet.

3 Bake in a preheated oven, 400°F/200°C, for 10 minutes, or until crisp and golden. Remove from the oven and immediately sprinkle over the Parmesan cheese. Serve the palmiers warm or transfer to a wire rack and let cool to room temperature. Garnish with sprigs of fresh basil.

cheese straws

ingredients

MAKES 24

4 oz/115 g/generous 3/4 cup
 all-purpose flour, plus
 extra for dusting
pinch of salt
1 tsp curry powder
2 oz/55 g butter, plus extra
 for greasing
2 oz/55 g/1/2 cup grated
 Cheddar cheese
1 egg, beaten
poppy and cumin seeds,
 for sprinkling

method

1 Sift the flour, salt, and curry powder into a bowl. Add the butter and rub in until the mixture resembles bread crumbs. Add the cheese and half the egg and mix to form a dough. Wrap in plastic wrap and chill in the refrigerator for 30 minutes.

2 Lightly grease several cookie sheets. On a floured counter, roll out the dough to 1/4-inch/5-mm thick. Cut into 3 x 1/2-inch/7.5 x 1-cm strips. Pinch the strips lightly along the sides and place on the prepared cookie sheets.

3 Brush the straws with the remaining egg and sprinkle half with poppy seeds and half with cumin seeds. Bake in a preheated oven, 400°F/200°C,for 10–15 minutes, or until golden. Transfer to wire racks to cool.

cheese & rosemary bites

ingredients

MAKES 40

8 oz/225 g cold butter, diced,
  plus extra for greasing
9 oz/250 g/1³/₄ cups
  all-purpose flour, plus
  extra for dusting
9 oz/250 g/2¹/₂ cups grated
  Gruyère cheese
¹/₂ tsp cayenne pepper
2 tsp finely chopped fresh
  rosemary leaves
1 egg yolk, beaten with
  1 tbsp water

method

1 Lightly grease 2 cookie sheets. Place the flour, butter, cheese, cayenne pepper, and chopped rosemary in a food processor. Pulse until the mixture forms a dough, adding a little cold water, if necessary, to bring the mixture together.

2 On a floured counter, roll out the dough to ¹/₄-inch/5-mm thick. Stamp out shapes such as stars and hearts with 2¹/₂-inch/6-cm cutters.

3 Place the shapes on the prepared cookie sheets, then cover with plastic wrap and let chill in the refrigerator for 30 minutes, or until firm. Brush with the beaten egg yolk and bake in a preheated oven, 350°F/180°C, for 10 minutes, or until golden brown. Let cool on the cookie sheets for 2 minutes, then serve warm or transfer to wire racks to cool.